Teach Meaningful

Teach Meaningful

Tools to Design the Curriculum at Your Core

Second Edition

LAUREN POROSOFF

ROWMAN & LITTLEFIELD
Lanham • Boulder • New York • London

Published by Rowman & Littlefield
An imprint of The Rowman & Littlefield Publishing Group, Inc.
4501 Forbes Boulevard, Suite 200, Lanham, Maryland 20706
www.rowman.com

6 Tinworth Street, London SE11 5AL, United Kingdom

British Library Cataloguing in Publication Information Available

Library of Congress Cataloging-in-Publication Data Is Available

ISBN 978-1-4758-5116-8 (cloth : alk. paper)
ISBN 978-1-4758-5117-5 (paperback : alk. paper)
ISBN 978-1-4758-5118-2 (electronic)

♾™ The paper used in this publication meets the minimum requirements of American
National Standard for Information Sciences—Permanence of Paper for Printed Library
Materials, ANSI/NISO Z39.48-1992.

Contents

List of Figures

Preface

The Values That Guided the Second Edition

Before I get to what's changed in this book, here's one thing that hasn't. It's still a book for teachers. The anthology *Poetry Speaks Who I Am* (Paschen & Raccah, 2010), which I used when I taught seventh-grade English, begins with the words "This is not a poetry anthology for adults, for children, for classroom study, or for required memorization and recitation. It's made just for you" (p. xiii). The book in your hands is not for administrators, for school officials, for mandatory in-service days, or for required adoption and implementation. It's for you.

I want this book to be applicable to you whatever grade and subject you teach, so I've done my best to provide examples and case studies from lots of grade levels and subject areas, including the subjects we typically call *academics* as well as music, the arts, and physical education. Because inclusion is important to me, I've tried to write about ideas that apply to all subjects and grade levels.

In the interest of conciseness, I don't always include multiple examples to illustrate a point, but I know it can be hard for, say, high school teachers to see themselves in a story about a second-grade teacher having his students make a dinosaur mural. Also, many of the stories in this book are based on what I've experienced in my classroom or witnessed firsthand at schools where I've worked, so middle school and humanities are overrepresented somewhat. I trust you to have the imagination and flexibility to see how the examples pertain to your work.

It's important to me that you be able to use what's in this book. Rather than leave you to sort out how to make the framework and examples work, I've included exercises, protocols, and templates to use alone and with colleagues to write and assess your curriculum. I created many of these tools for this new edition or adapted them from other books I've written, and I've revised all of the tools that appeared in the first edition to make them clearer and more useful.

One of the most noticeable differences between this edition and the first is the title. I called the first edition *Curriculum at Your Core*, an assertion that your teaching values matter even while you adhere to a set of standards such as the Common Core. But I'm not sure readers got that reference. Anyway, *Teach Meaningful* more accurately represents why I wrote this book. The new title uses disruptive grammar because it's meant to help you disrupt your curriculum's status quo. It's an incomplete thought, because we never complete the process of discovering and doing what matters, in the classroom or beyond.

Acknowledgments

This book never would have existed without the compassionate mentoring that Melanie Greenup gave me. She sent me to workshops, handed me books, and spent many hours talking to me so I'd develop the skills to write better curriculum and to support colleagues in writing theirs. Melanie sees clearly and almost clairvoyantly what people are supposed to do with their lives. I feel tremendously grateful for her wisdom and kindness, and I dedicate this book to her and to mentors like her.

Laurie Hornik is a brilliant teacher, a supportive colleague, and a kind friend. She shares her ideas generously and asks good questions, and she helps me return to my values and improve my practice. She also gave frequent and thoughtful (and sometimes funny) comments on even the bad early drafts of this book.

My co-everything, Dr. Jonathan Weinstein—besides being a loving partner and giving me the time and space to write—introduced me to contextual behavioral science, relational frame theory, and the way values are used in acceptance and commitment therapy. These became foundational ideas for this book, along with the books he and I have written together.

Workshops at the Bard Institute of Writing and Thinking, especially those that Dr. Carley Moore led, taught me ways teachers can discover and deepen their ideas. The exercises in this book that use writing as a means of thinking apply Bard Institute practices to curriculum design.

Eric Baylin and his colleagues at the Packer Collegiate Facilitative Leadership Institute taught me how critical friends' protocols encourage trust and inclusive participation among teachers who don't necessarily share values.

Matt and Jenn Villatte's extraordinary book and workshops cracked open contextual behavioral science for me. I'm forever their fan.

My former colleagues at the Charles E. Smith Jewish Day School, the Maret School, and the Ethical Culture Fieldston School inspired me with their excellent teaching. I thank them all, and especially those whose names and stories are used in this book: Ellie Bibas, Debbie Kriger, Laurie Hornik, Tony Marro, and Jeff Nurenberg. I also thank the colleagues who, over the years, worked closely with me on curriculum design: Mollie Sandberg, Dina Weinberg, Janet Goldschmidt, Kalin Taylor, Renee Charity Price, Lauren Keller, and Dori Kamlet Klar.

Thanks to my parents, Leslie and Harold Porosoff, and my children, Allison Porosoff and Jason Weinstein, for their love and support.

Finally, thanks to every student who's ever been in my class. I hope I taught them something they value.

Introduction

A Case for Values-Guided Curriculum Design

What brought you to teaching in the first place? What brings you back, day after day and year after year, to this difficult work? When your students finish a year with you, what do you most want them to take with them? When you retire, what do you want to have stood for? What do you want your teaching to *mean*?

Creating a curriculum means identifying the set of understandings and skills that are most important for students to learn—and what we deem "most important" depends on values. Teachers and administrators, missions and charters, school boards and standards committees, professional and parent associations, and the students themselves all make pronouncements about what they consider most important for students to learn. These are values statements.

This book is about how teachers, individually and in groups, can design more effective curriculum using their values as a starting place. But first, let's define what we mean by *values* and why getting clear on your values can help you design more meaningful units, courses, and programs.

WHAT VALUES ARE—AND AREN'T

Psychology professor Kelly Wilson defines values as "freely chosen, verbally constructed consequences of ongoing, dynamic, evolving patterns of activity, which establish predominant reinforcers for that activity that are intrinsic in engagement in the valued behavioral pattern itself" (Wilson & DuFrene,

2009, p. 64). This definition has been widely cited in books aimed at psychologists (Dahl, Lundgren, Plumb, & Stewart, 2009, p. 9; Hayes, Strosahl, & Wilson, 2012, pp. 92–93; Blackledge, 2015, p. 16; Tirch, Silberstein, & Kolts, 2015, p. 67; and Bennett & Oliver, 2019, p. 76).

But for purposes of considering how values impact curriculum design, we'll use a simplified and teaching-specific version of Wilson's technical definition: values are *qualities of action an educator thinks are important to make manifest in the classroom*. But even this simpler definition needs some analysis.

Values as Qualities of Action

As qualities of action, values answer questions about *how* we do things: *How will I teach? How will my students learn? How will we treat each other? How will we approach this topic? How will they approach the world after they develop these understandings?*

To name classroom actions, we need verbs such as *read, think, work, solve* problems, and *discuss* ideas. To name qualities of those actions—how we perform them—we need adverbs: read *curiously*, think *creatively*, work *attentively*, solve problems *resourcefully*, discuss ideas *respectfully*. But sometimes adverbs sound a little clunky, and it's easier to say, "I value *creativity*" or "I value *being creative*" than "I value *behaving creatively*."

Appendix A (p. 187) has examples of values, phrased as abstract nouns such as *creativity, curiosity*, and *resourcefulness*. As you think about values, though, realize that they are not things you can have or states you can achieve, but qualities you can bring to your actions at any time. You might say, for example, "I'm not creative," or "Creativity isn't my strong suit," but you still can choose to teach creatively, and you can design learning experiences that foster creativity in your students.

Values as What the Educator Thinks Are Important

Individuals get to choose their own values. Whatever makes teaching and learning meaningful to you will be different from what's meaningful to your colleagues and administrators, to your students and their parents, to the architects of state tests and national standards, and to the author of this book. Clarifying *your* values—the qualities of action *you* think are important—will help you design curriculum that serves those values, as well as the values of others who have a stake in what students learn.

If your focus is on meeting standards and raising test scores, you might be skeptical about the place of *your* values in planning curriculum. The very idea of talking about your values might sound lofty, cute, or pointless—especially if your job and your school's funding are on the line. You stick to the standards and let them tell you what to cover in your class.

But for one thing, no matter how standards-compliant or prescribed your curriculum is, you're the person in the classroom with the students, and your values come through. You teach who you are, and you matter.

For another, meeting externally created standards doesn't have to mean ignoring your own values. Education professor Christine Sleeter (2005) distinguishes between "standards-driven" and "standards-conscious" curriculum planning. In standards-driven planning, the teacher treats the standards as if they *are* the curriculum and tries to get through them all before test time, whereas in standards-conscious planning, "the standards are a tool, but not the starting point, and do not define the central organizing ideas and ideology of one's curriculum" (Sleeter, 2005, p. 60).

We can think of the standards the way we'd think of a nutrition guide. Nutrition guides tell us how much of each nutrient we need, but they don't tell us what to make for dinner. In planning a meal, we might pull out a favorite recipe, see which vegetables are in season, or grab whatever's on sale at the market. *Then*, we consider whether the meal we've planned gives us the protein and vitamins we need, and we make any necessary adjustments.

Curriculum planning can work in much the same way. Instead of starting with a set of standards, start with your values. What concepts and processes do you think are most important for your students to understand? What academic, relational, and practical skills do they need? What kinds of experiences will help them learn what matters most? Then, as you plan your unit, consult the standards to make sure you're meeting them, and adjust your teaching accordingly.

Making Values Manifest in a Classroom

In our classrooms, our values help guide the actions we choose for *ourselves*—how *we* want to teach. But as teachers, we also have a profound influence on our *students'* actions. Every time we give directions, ask a question, set up the classroom furniture, hand out materials, post information, design a lesson or assignment, offer feedback, speak up or stay silent, we influence how our students act. Of course, we're not the only source of influence; how our students learn, work, and interact also depends upon physiological, psychological, historical, cultural, economic, and environmental factors beyond our control—and often beyond theirs, too. Still, our actions influence theirs.

As you consider your teaching, you might find it useful to distinguish between your *first-degree values* (how *you* want to approach your teaching) and *second-degree values* (how you want *your students* to approach their learning). This book is about how teachers can design curriculum that encourages students to understand material, develop skills, create work products, and build relationships that you, the teacher, consider important. That's why when we refer to your values, we usually mean your second-degree values: what matters to you in how your students approach their learning.

How Values Differ from Goals and Preferences

Because values are desirable qualities of action, people sometimes confuse them with desirable outcomes of action (goals) and desirable qualities of an experience (preferences). Psychologists who write about values often distinguish between values and goals (Hayes, Strosahl, & Wilson, 2012; Harris, 2009; Wilson & DuFrene, 2009; Wilson & Murrell, 2004). Unlike goals, which can be checked off a to-do list, values are ongoing.

For example, math teacher Beatriz T. Font Strawhun had her sixth graders analyze school overcrowding by calculating the area of classroom space per student at their school and comparing their results to data from other schools (Turner & Font Strawhun, 2007). Creating this project was a goal. Once her students completed the project, the teacher was done. However, if she wanted to make sure her students "used rigorous mathematics to investigate . . . issues about the school and local community that concerned them" (Turner & Font Strawhun, 2007, p. 458), that's a value—an ongoing process she could engage in every day.

Values also aren't mere preferences. Teaching by your values means you create opportunities for students to engage in learning processes and reach outcomes you believe to be important. The fact that you enjoy doing a certain activity or discussing a particular topic with your class doesn't necessarily mean your students are doing important work. Living by your values often brings deep satisfaction and vitality, but the day-to-day effort of committing to values doesn't necessarily feel pleasant and sometimes feels like a burden (Yadavaia & Hayes, 2009).

Let's say that a high-school history teacher values clear communication and continual growth. In long comments on students' research papers, he points out specific examples of where they have and haven't been clear and suggests strategies for improving clarity in future writing. All of that commenting can feel tedious, but the teacher is pursuing his values: when his students write their next papers, they consult his comments, apply his suggestions, and grow in their ability to communicate clearly.

Conversely, if this same teacher enjoys the feeling of being the center of attention, he might tell funny stories in class. Though he delights in hearing his students laugh and gasp, he's not necessarily pursuing his teaching values in those moments. In fact, if he spends so much time telling stories that his students miss opportunities to develop their own communication skills, then the teacher's pursuit of his own good feelings gets in the way of pursuing his values.

Now that we've explored what values are—qualities of action you think are important, if not always pleasant, to make manifest in your classroom every day—let's turn to why becoming more aware of your values can help you design better curriculum.

CURRICULUM AS COHERENCE

In designing curriculum, your task is to make sense out of a seemingly infinite set of possibilities. Which topics should you teach? In what order? How much time should you devote to each one? Which skills will prepare your students for the future, and which skills do they need right now? Which instructional methods and resources will you use? How will you assess your students' learning? What kinds of work products will they make? When will you incorporate relational and self-reflective skills? How will you teach cultural, digital, financial, and ecological literacies? What about practical skills such as navigating a city bus system or fixing a leaky pipe? All of these are values questions, to which standards and curriculum guides offer few answers.

Meanwhile, every day new books and videos come out. Problems emerge that we need to analyze logically and process emotionally. Our classes are canceled for snowstorms and standardized tests. And a class of thirty students has thirty different ways of understanding the world. How do we make sense of all of that?

According to psychology professors Matthieu Villatte, Jennifer Villatte, and Steven Hayes (2016), we have three distinct ways we make sense of the world, or create *coherence* among our experiences:

1. In *essential* coherence, we match things in the world to a predefined image (as when we decide an animal is a duck when it walks and quacks like one).
2. In *social* coherence, we select actions based on whether others will approve (as when we imagine how our friends might react to the haircut we're thinking of getting).
3. In *functional* coherence, we see how well an idea works for a particular purpose (as when we use the side of a book to draw a straight line, even though that's not how we typically use a book).

The type of coherence we create—how we make sense of all of the stuff we might teach—will profoundly influence our curriculum.

Essential Coherence

We create essential coherence when we match things in the world to a preexisting image. Curriculum has essential coherence when it resembles something already defined as *the curriculum*. Whether our images come from our own childhoods, our schools' or disciplines' traditions, or exemplars of twenty-first-century education, modeling our practices after these images saves us time and energy. If we always take the same route to work—or always teach a unit the same way—we can turn our attention to the million other decisions we have to make.

The problem with essential coherence is that when we adhere to a rule, role, or tradition, we become less sensitive to changes around us that might make a different behavior more effective (Hayes, 1989; Villatte, Villatte, & Hayes, 2016). Let's take the example of commuting to school. You probably have a route you typically take. If *going to school* has become synonymous with *taking this particular route*, you might not think to check for a road closure or a fare increase. By the time you notice those changes, you're stuck. And if you only focus on getting to school quickly, you might not notice other possible functions of your commute, such as self-care or socializing, and ignore alternatives such as carpooling with colleagues, or taking a longer walk that allows you to exercise and listen to a favorite podcast.

Similarly, we can get stuck in narrow and rigid perceptions of our curriculum, limiting our ability to notice new, more effective possibilities. How would you fill in the blanks in some of the following sentences?

- At [insert the name of your school], we've always taught ___.
- In [insert your subject], students have to learn ___.
- Every school in [insert your state] has a ___ program.
- It wouldn't be a [insert the name of your school] education without ___.
- If I got rid of ___, I wouldn't be able to call myself a [insert your subject area and grade level] teacher.

What other images do you associate with your curriculum—whether they come from colleagues, administrators, professional literature, or popular media? When they, or you, define *the* curriculum, how might that definition limit your awareness of what *else* might be possible in your subject and for your students?

As we'll see, understanding our values can help us overcome rigid perceptions of our curriculum so that we can notice possibilities beyond what our roles and traditions dictate. When we clarify what matters to us as teachers, *anything* that meaningfully moves our students toward what's important becomes a possibility. Even if we stick with the same curriculum we've always taught, we're no longer doing it because that's just what we do; we're doing it because it makes important learning happen.

Social Coherence

Another way we make sense of the world is through social coherence, or doing whatever helps us look good, sound smart, fit in, or otherwise gain or maintain our status in a group. Imagine that you start carpooling to school with three colleagues. On your day to drive, you open a traffic app to find the fastest route, but one of your colleagues tells you to turn it off because he knows a shortcut. If your experience tells you that the app works better, but you turn it off anyway, that's social coherence: your action makes sense as a way to preserve your colleague's self-confidence and prevent unnecessary conflict. If you then hit traffic and your other two colleagues start mercilessly teasing the one who suggested the shortcut, that's *also* social coherence, because they're doing something mean just to amuse each other.

As teachers, we might make certain curricular choices based less on our values than on pleasing, impressing, or placating others—and with good reason. If we don't measure up to our administrators' standards, then we might lose our jobs. If we never yield to our colleagues, then we destroy our relationships. And if we make students or their parents unhappy, then they might make us even unhappier. Anyone who works in a group sometimes goes along to get along. It's when we make pleasing others and gaining status our primary goal that we can lose sight of what matters—in the curriculum and in the relationship itself.

What topics, assignments, classroom practices, or resources would you put into the blanks in these sentences?

- I don't love teaching ___, but it's not worth fighting with my colleagues about it.
- Sometimes I let the kids ___, even if it's not the absolute best way for them to learn.
- If I want to look good in front of my principal, I make sure to ___.
- Parents would complain if we stopped teaching ___.
- In order to keep up with our peer schools, we have to ___.

Again, try to think of more examples of how you (or others) use certain content, methods, or assignments in order to gain acceptance or approval. Does the resulting curriculum best promote student learning? Instead of trying to look a certain way—smart, competent, professional, rigorous, fun, friendly, agreeable, right—we can notice and name common values. Even if we disagree with colleagues or other stakeholders about what the curriculum should *look like*, we can look for places where we agree on what the curriculum should *do*.

Functional Coherence

A third way we make sense of the world is through *functional* coherence, or doing what works. What we think works best will depend on what matters most to us in that moment. Let's say we're trying to decide on the best way to get to school. Is the best way the fastest way? The cheapest way? The way that takes you past your favorite coffee shop? The way that has the lowest carbon footprint, or that gives you exercise, or that provides social connection? Depending on where you live, many different routes might serve several of these purposes, to varying degrees. You might look for a compromise between different values, or you might prioritize different values on different days. And even when you know which values you want to serve with your commute, you still need to map out exactly how to get from point A to point B.

Similarly, we might think of many different ways to create a workable unit. Designing a functionally coherent unit means deciding between these alternatives. What is the unit's primary purpose? Which lessons and activities best serve that purpose? Are there activities that don't serve the primary purpose but are worthwhile detours? How much time should this unit take, and how much time should be reserved for other units? Although values clarification alone won't answer these questions for us—any more than knowing *how* we want to travel to school will tell us *which* route to take—our values do give us a way to assess our options.

HOW TO USE THIS BOOK

Getting clear on your values—as an individual teacher and as a member of a department, team, school, district, and profession—gives you a starting place to design curriculum that ensures meaningful learning.

This book's first two chapters adapt practices from contextual psychology to help clarify the values you want to bring to your curriculum and overcome barriers to values-congruent teaching, both as an individual teacher (chapter 1) and within a group of teachers who work together (chapter 2). Note, however, that values clarification is an iterative process: understanding your values will help you design curriculum, but designing curriculum will help you understand the values that you can then bring to future units.

The next four chapters show you how to design an academic unit of study, using individual or group's values as a starting place. We'll explore how to imagine new possibilities for your units (chapter 3), select and articulate a focus for a unit (chapter 4), design and sequence lessons within the unit (chapter 5), and assess students' knowledge and skills during the unit (chapter 6).

The last two chapters account for how curriculum design becomes more complex when units come together to form entire courses (chapter 7) and cross disciplines (chapter 8).

Each chapter concludes with three tools—either individual exercises or group protocols—to help you expand your awareness of curricular possibilities, make values-consistent design choices, and collaborate with colleagues whose values might be different from yours—all so you can design more meaning-ful learning experiences for your students. The individual exercises ask you to imagine curricular possibilities or assess existing curriculum by yourself, although you and a partner or group could do any of these exercises simul-taneously and then discuss your responses. The group protocols encourage inclusive participation and critical reflection so that you and your colleagues can work together toward more cohesive curriculum you can all stand behind.

1

Discover the Values That Guide Your Teaching

Imagine that you're attending a summer institute on teaching academic content through the arts. In one workshop, each teacher researches an animal from the Chesapeake Bay—you're assigned the menhaden—in order to make a collaborative mural. Together, you and the other teachers paint a huge piece of particleboard with alternating streaks of blue and green so it looks like water. Then, you make line drawings of your animals, trace the drawings onto transparencies so you can project them onto the water background, retrace them there, and paint them. You show interrelationships by painting predators lurking by their prey and symbiotic organisms helping each other. The mural is stunning, and in the process of making it, you find yourself learning a lot about the Bay.

That night at dinner, you meet Henry, a second-grade teacher from Washington, D.C. He's chattering excitedly about an idea he got from the workshop. At his school, second graders begin the year with a unit on dinosaurs. What if his students were to form three groups and create a three-panel mural of the Triassic, Jurassic, and Cretaceous periods? Each student could research and paint a different dinosaur. His students could look at impression fossils to learn what their dinosaurs' skin and feathers should look like, and because there's no way to know what colors dinosaurs were, the students could research birds—dinosaurs' closest living relatives—to get ideas. They also could research plants from the Triassic, Jurassic, and Cretaceous periods to include in their mural panels. Groups would have to decide together how to depict their dinosaurs' relationships to one another and to their habitat.

Henry talks about this project with a growing sense of vitality and purpose. The mural would engage his students so much more than the worksheets he'd handed out in the past. Students would learn key science concepts while also thinking creatively. The project would provide an authentic reason for students to ask research questions, read for information, and think critically. There'd be a balance of individual and collaborative decision making. Everyone would participate and make a unique contribution to the group. And at the end, the class would have a beautiful mural to remind them of their shared learning. Doing this sort of work with students was why Henry became a teacher in the first place. The project reflects his values.

Henry realizes that he's been talking for quite a while and asks, "What about you? Does a mural sound like something you could do with your class?"

As a thought experiment, imagine how you could use this project, even if you don't think you would. If you were to have your students create a mural to learn content in your course, what content would you use it to teach? How would you divide up the work? What would your students learn from doing it? What would you have to do to make a mural work in your space, with your population, and in a reasonable time frame? On the other hand, how might this project get in the way of student learning? What important lessons and assignments wouldn't you give up to do a mural? What kind of environment have you worked hard to create in your classroom that this project might threaten or subvert?

How you answer questions like these depends, at least in part, on your values. (Even *whether* you answered these questions depends in part on your values.) Precisely because most academic teachers don't use muraling as a teaching tool, imagining how you could use the project, and why you might not, helps you see your class from a different perspective. Based on your responses, what would you say some of your teaching values are? That is, what qualities of action are important for your students to bring to their learning, work, and relationships in your class?

If imagining the mural project didn't get you very far, try using some of the following questions to take different perspectives on your curriculum in order to identify some of the values you want to bring to it:

- Imagine your retirement party. What do you hope your colleagues and administrators will say in their speeches?
- Imagine it's the last day of school, and you receive the thank-you note you most wish a student or parent would write. Who wrote it? What does it say?
- Think of a few former students who struggled in your class. What did you teach these students that you most hope they're still using?
- What have some of your colleagues done in their classes that you disapproved of or resisted? What would you have done differently if you'd been teaching their classes?
- Who is a colleague you look up to? What does this colleague do that inspires you? What are this colleague's strengths that you admire?
- Make a list of "magic moments" in your classroom.
- Imagine that you visit a school that's very similar to yours, except for one difference that greatly impacts students for the better. What's the difference, and what's better for students because of it?
- Look around your classroom. What do you see that brings you a sense of vitality or purpose?

Writing about your work from another person's perspective—whether it's a student, parent, colleague, or administrator—might free you to say things you wouldn't want to say about yourself because it would feel like bragging. Imagining a different time, such as the end of the year or even the end of your career, lets you clear away the moment-to-moment challenges of your school life and pay attention to what you truly want to stand for as a teacher. And imagining other places, such as a colleague's classroom or another school, helps you notice what's important in yours.

In answering some of these questions, you might have noticed some discomfort. For example, when recalling a student who struggled, maybe you felt a little disappointed in yourself, or angry at a situation that kept you from meeting this student's needs. Or when thinking of colleagues who inspire you, perhaps you felt guilty that you're not living up to some standard you think they set, or perhaps you felt defensive about your own practices. Or maybe it felt awkward to identify colleagues whose practices you oppose, or aspects of your school you wish were different. But if you feel uncomfortable, that's a sign that your values are at stake. What are some of those values?

BARRIERS TO VALUES-CONSISTENT TEACHING

After the mural workshop, Henry jots down some ideas for his dinosaur unit. As much as he loves the summer, he can hardly wait for September to come. Then, September does come.

Henry's feelings of vitality and purpose give way to anxiety and doubt. *I don't have the time to do such a huge project. I have so much other stuff to cover. Plus, it sounds like a lot of work to get all of those supplies. I can't even fit one piece of particleboard in my car, let alone three. All of this will cost money my school doesn't have. Anyway, the other second-grade teachers won't want to do this. And if I try to do it myself, they'll say I'm not a team player. And my principal will be on my case about the three giant boards taking up space in my room, and about the paint I need to make sure I clean up. Forget it. We can make dinosaur A-to-Z booklets like we always have. They work just fine.*

Author Russ Harris (2009) identifies four kinds of barriers to values-consistent living: (1) getting stuck in self-limiting beliefs, (2) disregarding what matters most, (3) avoiding discomfort, and (4) external circumstances. Let's see how these barriers might impact teaching and learning.

Getting Stuck in Self-Limiting Beliefs

People think self-limiting thoughts all the time. We believe we can't do something that matters to us because of a deficit within ourselves: *I don't have the experience to make this work*, or *I'm just not a creative type*. Or we think some aspect of our personal or professional identities conflicts with the action we want to take: *Math teachers don't teach writing*, or *I don't do that touchy-feely stuff*.

It doesn't matter whether these self-limiting thoughts are true; what matters is whether we let these thoughts stop us from teaching by our values. Maybe it's *true* that Henry isn't talented artistically, all the know-how he has about muraling comes from a single workshop, and his second-grade colleagues usually reject his ideas. But even if our self-limiting beliefs are *true*, we can choose to act in accordance with our values.

A belief about ourselves also doesn't have to be negative to be limiting. Imagine if Henry had thoughts such as *Our dinosaur unit is already one of the kids' favorites. Anyway, I'm a better artist than the kids. They'll be intimidated when they see my example.* These beliefs are positive in a certain sense, but they could still get in Henry's way—unless he chose to believe them while going ahead with the mural.

What thoughts do you have about yourself—your role, your skills, your personality—that might hold you back from teaching by your values?

Disregarding What Matters Most

Henry tries to convince himself that the students will be fine making A-to-Z booklets; surely, they learned *something* last year and weren't *harmed* by the project. Though the booklets aren't a collaborative project, he reasons, some students prefer to work alone, and though making a picture book of alphabetized dinosaurs doesn't show which dinosaurs lived at which times or how they interacted with their surroundings, it helps kids develop language skills. Right?

By telling himself these stories, Henry tries to ignore how much he cares about innovation, authenticity, engagement, collaboration, and transferability—but deep down, he knows the mural project would better serve these values.

What stories have you told yourself to explain why you're not teaching in a way that would serve your values? Even if those stories are true, how helpful are they?

Avoiding Uncomfortable Feelings

Feelings such as frustration, embarrassment, and exhaustion aren't fun, but they're sometimes a necessary part of living by our values. Setting up a mural project would take Henry's time and effort—to go to the hardware store, haul the materials to school, tape garbage bags to the floor to protect it from paint, find resources about Mesozoic flora and fauna, put students into groups, and deal with both the inevitable "I wanted the apatosaurus!" tantrum and his colleagues' quiet hostility if he does the mural without their blessing. Using the booklet project would let him avoid these annoyances and fears, but avoiding these feelings would also mean avoiding his values.

What uncomfortable feelings—such as frustration, worry, boredom, or annoyance—might be getting in the way of values-consistent teaching for you?

External Factors

Humans are endlessly creative in the face of external barriers. Is there no way for Henry to get that wood to school? If he physically won't be able to teach with three giant boards in his classroom, does the building have another place that could accommodate them? Are there lessons Henry could shorten or eliminate to make room for the mural in his schedule? If his school lacks the money and resources to make this project work, could he apply for a grant, raise funds in the community, or come up with a lower-cost alternative such as making a sidewalk mural with chalk? If his principal seems hesitant, could he start a conversation with her about the benefits of teaching through the arts?

When people find reasons not to teach by their values, they often see these reasons as external—no time, no money, no space, no support—without realizing or acknowledging how many of these barriers are inside them. It isn't impossible for Henry to get the materials, space, and time he needs for his dinosaur mural. It's just hard.

Despite the barriers, Henry knows that his students would learn more from making the mural than from making booklets. So, he borrows a friend's truck, drives it to the hardware store, and gets help moving the materials. He asks his principal to help him find a place where the mural won't be in anyone's way, and she suggests a hallway that works perfectly. His colleagues are indeed mad when he does the mural after they all said they didn't want to do it too, but he lives with their disapproval, and eventually they get over it. The students love the project and learn a lot about the Mesozoic era, the research process, collaboration, and self-expression.

What about you? What external barriers have you encountered to values-consistent teaching? What creative workarounds might there be? Who can help you?

TOOLS FOR DISCOVERING THE VALUES THAT GUIDE YOUR TEACHING

The remainder of this chapter consists of three exercises designed to help you more deeply understand the values you want to bring to curriculum design. In *Rate Your Teacher*, you'll identify criteria that matter most to you when defining teaching excellence. *Three Ups Three Downs* asks you first to identify some of your values in the abstract, and then to identify concrete examples of how you make these values manifest in your work. In *Values Rendering*, you'll choose a piece of your work and discover what values it communicates, and then decide if these are the values you want to keep choosing.

Although these exercises involve your individual values, you might invite a few of your colleagues to complete them, too. Afterward, you can look for values you all share. Or try the exercises on your own as a way to reflect on the qualities you want to bring to your teaching.

Rate Your Teacher

The website RateMyTeachers.com invites students to post anonymously about how good they think their teachers are. On a scale of one to five, students rate their teachers in six categories—clarity, easiness, exam difficulty, helpfulness, knowledge, and textbook use—and can add comments.

Students have many fewer formal opportunities to evaluate us than we have to evaluate them. Yet the RateMyTeachers system in many ways resembles assessment systems in schools. The people being assessed don't get to choose when, how, or by whom they're assessed, and a complex endeavor is reduced to a few numbers and a brief comment.

But surely not everyone would consider clarity, easiness, exam difficulty, helpfulness, knowledge, and textbook use to be the six most important qualities of a teacher. For example, does every teacher want to be easy? Maybe we don't want the material to be unnecessarily tedious or confusing, but surely some of us strive to challenge our students with complex real-world tasks and rigorous critical analysis. Students who, for example, create animations juxtaposing the language in a Shakespearean monologue with pictures from the news, or decompose the function $f(x) = (x + 1)^2$, or analyze climate injustices from an intersectional feminist perspective, might not find these tasks easy or fun, but does that mean the task wasn't worthwhile? Do teachers who assign such tasks deserve low ratings because they're not easy?

When we set criteria to rate something—whether it's a student's work or a teacher's—we articulate our values. The designers of RateMyTeachers.com must consider teachers good when they're easy. At least, that's a teaching criterion they assume students would find important. But if *you* were to choose the criteria by which your students would rate you, you might choose differently—and in choosing, you'd learn something about your values.

In this exercise, *Rate Your Teacher*, you'll choose six criteria that you would use to have your students rate you. Choosing criteria doesn't mean you have to ask your students to rate you—although you could if you want that information. But the point here is simply to ask yourself which criteria you'd find most important. Choosing six criteria might be difficult, but it will help you articulate the values you most want to commit to as you design learning experiences for your students.

Individual Exercise

1. Appendix A (p. 187) has examples of values: qualities some people think are important to bring to their actions. Use these examples to help you make a list of qualities you find important to bring to your classroom. If there's a quality you want to embody but that isn't written, feel free to write it in.

2. Imagine that your students were going to rate you, as a teacher, on six of the criteria you just identified. For which six would it be most important to you to get high ratings from your students? Write these six in the Key Ratings chart (figure 1.1, below). Note that the purpose of creating this instrument isn't necessarily to *use* it—although you can—but rather to clarify your values as a teacher.

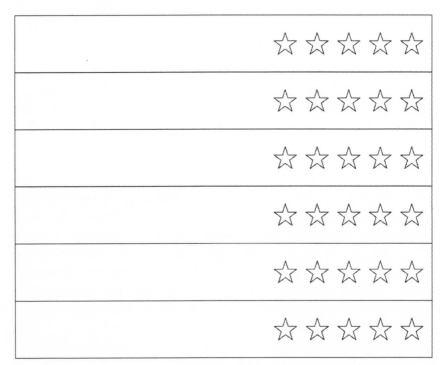

FIGURE 1.1
Key Ratings

Reflection Questions

- Why did you choose these six?
- For which of your six criteria do you think your current students would rate you highly? What makes you think so?
- How do you bring these qualities to different aspects of your teaching? Consider, for example, how you enact these qualities in designing lessons and units, explaining new material, managing your classroom, assessing students' learning, giving feedback, or building community among your students.
- Of these six areas, in which one do you most want to grow? When you think about how you want to bring this quality to your teaching, what's something new you'd like to try? When will you try it? Who can help?
- Thinking back on your career as an educator, how have you grown in these six areas?

Variation

Although (mercifully) no such site as RateMyColleagues exists, you could repeat this exercise, but consider instead what you find important to bring to your working relationships with the adults at your school.

Three Ups Three Downs

As teachers, enacting our values means more than choosing how *we* act in the classroom. We also work to create a context for our *students'* actions. For this exercise, *Three Ups Three Downs*, you'll identify qualities you think are most important for your students to bring to their learning, their work, and their relationships. Then, you'll think of specific times when you succeeded and struggled to elicit these qualities in your students, and write about these times in the Teaching Ups and Downs chart (figure 1.2, p. 10).

The goal here is not to wallow in your failures or even to celebrate your successes, but rather to clarify the kinds of learning conditions you want to create for your students and discover how you can make your lessons, assignments, and classroom routines even more meaningful in the future.

Individual Exercise

1. Look at the qualities of action listed in appendix A (p. 187). Identify a quality you want students to bring to their *learning*, and label it *L*; a quality you

A specific lesson that successfully brought out my students' (L) _____:	A specific lesson that failed to bring out my students' (L) _____:
An assignment that successfully brought out my students' (W) _____:	An assignment that failed to bring out my students' (W) _____:
A classroom routine that successfully brought out my students' (R) _____:	A classroom routine that failed to bring out my students' (R) _____:

FIGURE 1.2
Teaching Ups and Downs

want students to bring to their *work*, and label it *W*; and a quality you want students to bring to their *relationships* with one another, and label it *R*. If a quality that matters to you isn't written, feel free to write it in and label it.

2. Look at the Teaching Ups and Downs chart (figure 1.2, p. 10). In both columns, the letters *L*, *W*, and *R* appear beside blanks. Copy the values you labeled with those letters onto the respective lines. You'll copy each value twice, so all three appear on both sides of the chart.

3. Think of times when you successfully got your students to bring these qualities to their learning, work, and relationships. Try to think of a specific lesson, assignment, and classroom routine that promoted actions consistent with these values, and write brief descriptions in the appropriate boxes.

4. Think of times when you struggled or failed to get your students to bring these qualities to their learning, work, and relationships. Try to think of a specific lesson, assignment, and classroom routine that somehow prevented or discouraged actions consistent with these values. Write brief descriptions in the appropriate boxes.

Reflection Questions
- Which skills did you learn from your successes? From your struggles?
- What did you learn about yourself from your successes? From your struggles?
- How can you create more opportunities for students to enact the three values you identified as important?
- What obstacles make it difficult for you to bring out the qualities you think are important for your students to enact? Is it a lack of time? Resources? Experience? Planning? Agency? Something else? How can your colleagues and administrators support you in overcoming some of these obstacles?

Extension

After you describe your successes and struggles, find work you've created—such as lesson plans, slides, behavioral guidelines, assignment guidelines, or rubrics—that illustrate your three successes and your three struggles. You also could take photos of student work or classroom displays that show how you succeeded and struggled. Assemble this work in some way, perhaps by putting the work into a single binder, or by linking each piece to a single online document. You can keep this compilation to yourself and use it only to clarify your values, or you can use it to start conversations with administrators and colleagues about how you can make your work more values-consistent in the future.

Values Rendering

In digital photography, *rendering* is the electronic processing of a data file to produce a visual image. Sometimes when the file is large, rendering the image takes a few moments, and we watch it turn from pixels into something recognizable. In this exercise, you'll render your values from a piece of your work—a text such as an assignment, lesson plan, or website; or a physical space you read as if it were a text, such as a bulletin board or display, or even your classroom itself. As best you can, try to read what the work *actually says*, as opposed to what you intended to communicate.

Individual Exercise
1. Select a piece of your work, such as an assignment, lesson plan, rubric, slide show, website, bulletin board, or area of your classroom.
2. List specific features of this work. Notice details, and notice more details, without interpretation or judgment. Look for the nonobvious. What's here that you hadn't paid much attention to until now?
3. List questions you have about this piece of work as a whole, any part of it, or its layout. You might have questions about things from your first list, and you might have questions about new things you notice as you continue to look. You might find yourself imagining answers to some of your questions, or you might have no idea. But don't write down questions you already know the answers to.
4. Based on your two lists, write a response to the question "What does this work communicate about what success means in my class?"

Reflection Questions
- What does this piece of work *do*? What actions does it encourage or discourage?
- Who is this work for? Who isn't it for?
- How might social identifiers such as race, gender, socioeconomic status, first language, and ability impact a student's experience of this work?
- How do you want to define *success* in your class, according to your values?

Variation

Values Rendering asks you to view your own work with openness and curiosity, almost as if you've never seen it before. But because setting aside our biases is challenging, and perhaps impossible, an even better way to do this exercise is to get together with a colleague you trust and render the values from each other's work. You might be surprised by what someone else sees, the questions they ask, and the definition of success they infer. How does this person's interpretation compare to the message you intended to send? How does it compare to the message you want to send? How can you and your colleague help each other to enact your values more fully in your work?

ONWARD

This chapter included various ways to clarify your values as an individual teacher. In the next chapter, we'll turn to how groups of teachers can clarify values they share.

2

Discover Your Team's Shared Values

Jill, Vita, and Kenny teach eighth-grade English. Their next unit is on Anzia Yezierska's *Bread Givers* (2003/1923), a story set in the 1920s on Manhattan's Lower East Side, about a working-class Jewish girl who ultimately defies her demanding parents. Jill calls *Bread Givers* a "girl book" and wants to make sure to engage the boys in her class. She typically ends the unit with a mock trial where the parents are charged with abuse. Students of all genders love playing the roles of lawyers and book characters, and the trial format taps into different students' strengths while ensuring that everyone analyzes the book closely.

Vita is entering her second year at the school, and when she read *Bread Givers*, she noticed how it perpetuates stereotypes about Jews, the working class, and women. She wishes her department would reconsider the entire book list in terms of cultural relevance, but she doesn't want to say anything because she's still new to the school. In the meantime, she decides that her students will discuss stereotypes in the text and then make videos analyzing stereotypes in more current media. She hopes to move through the unit quickly, though, because last year she struggled to cover the grammar she was supposed to teach, and she also wants her students to do more independent reading.

Kenny has been teaching at the school for twenty-six years and brought *Bread Givers* into the curriculum, back when eighth graders learned about immigrant populations in their history class. Kenny, who also teaches tenth-grade honors English, wants to make sure his eighth graders gain the necessary critical reading and analytical writing skills for high school. His units, including this one, usually end with students writing essays about a theme or symbol in the book they've just read.

Kenny, Vita, and Jill all get good evaluations from their principal, and they all can point to standards they address in their versions of the *Bread Givers* unit. When they share their ideas for the unit at a department meeting, each says that the other two approaches sound great—but that they'll stick with their own.

We're imagining three eighth-grade English teachers, but we could just as easily imagine members of a high-school science department, or a fourth-grade team, or even a whole school having similar conflicts when they're expected to teach the same content and skills but bring different values to their work.

VALUES-CONSCIOUS COLLABORATION

Suppose that Jill, Vita, and Kenny meet to discuss the upcoming *Bread Givers* unit, each bringing a very different idea of which themes and skills they'll emphasize, and which lessons and assignments they'll give. If they only share their plans and not their underlying values, then here's what could happen.

- They politely agree to disagree. Jill does the trial, Vita does the stereotype videos, and Kenny does the traditional essays. Their students benefit from their strengths as individual teachers but not from their collective strengths.
- The three teachers argue over which approach is best. They all cite research and expert opinions to support their positions but undermine their relationships and ultimately their program.
- They agree to use some of each teacher's ideas in creating a common experience for all eighth graders. For example, all eighth graders could spend one class period discussing stereotypes in the book and comparing these to media stereotypes, then put on a mini-trial, and then write essays about themes. This hodgepodge version of the unit lacks purpose and cohesiveness, and each teacher feels rushed and dissatisfied.
- Two teachers go along with the third's plan. The group doesn't necessarily pick the best plan; the two teachers who agree to it might just have less power, or less energy to argue. This approach probably will breed resentment.

- Two teachers agree to a version of the unit that incorporates both sets of ideas—for example, Vita and Kenny decide that their students will write essays analyzing stereotypes in the book—leaving the third teacher to go along with that plan or separate from the group. This approach probably will also breed resentment as well as exclusion.

Now imagine that instead of focusing on the form their unit takes, the three teachers listen for what matters to each of them. Underneath their different approaches are some of the same values: they all want their students to read closely and critically, to engage fully, and to build skills they'll need for their futures. Noticing and naming these common values would help these teachers defuse tension, proceed from a place of mutual respect, and possibly discover a way to combine their approaches without sacrificing what's most important.

For example, what if they were to create a unit on how books both perpetuate and challenge stereotypes? Their students could analyze the ways *Bread Givers*, and other more contemporary texts, do both. Then, they could put the book itself on trial for perpetuating stereotypes. After the trial, they could write essays analyzing a particular stereotype in the text. But even if Jill, Vita, and Kenny still ended up teaching different units, talking about their values would help them develop a healthy working relationship, appreciate each other's strengths, and learn from one another. Accounting for multiple sets of values makes the curriculum design process more complicated, but getting other perspectives and ideas can be rewarding for you and ultimately for your students.

DISCOVERING SHARED VALUES

If we care about our students and their learning, we might feel angry if a colleague dismisses our good ideas, afraid that a particular lesson might not work, or sad if our students' work falls short of our expectations. When we talk about our values, we invite our emotions into the room, too. As psychology professor Kelly Wilson puts it, "Values and vulnerabilities are poured from the same vessel" (Wilson & DuFrene, 2009, p. 8). When we care, we open ourselves to anger, fear, sadness, disappointment, embarrassment, frustration—and also to joy, fulfillment, and vitality.

However, in our workplace we're supposed to remain cool, calm, and dispassionate—and not show too much emotion. Anger might make us look unprofessional. Our colleagues might interpret fear as a sign of incompetence.

One person's display of sadness might make everyone else feel awkward. Showing emotion might invoke our colleagues' judgment, as well as biases based on our years of experience, gender, race, and other social identifiers.

To explore values in a group at work, we need to create safety for everyone so we can maintain our professional boundaries while opening up about what matters to us. To make authentic sharing safer and more inclusive within the professional environment, we can do the following:

1. Assume diverse thinking about even the most fundamental aspects of teaching and learning.
2. Clarify curricular decision-making processes so teachers know when they have autonomy, when they must come to a consensus, and who resolves conflicts.
3. Structure communication to create safety and inclusion.
4. When exploring values, make that process itself the only outcome of the work.

Assume Diverse Thinking

Schools are complicated social institutions with potential conflict at every level. Maybe you've watched school leaders' efforts to force change or create buy-in met with reluctant compliance or vocal resistance. We might assume that teachers either subscribe to their school's stated values or at least agree to teach by them, but the mere fact of working together at the same school doesn't mean agreeing on even the most fundamental aspects of teaching.

Take, for example, the following four curriculum values orientations, adapted from the work of education professor Michael Schiro (2013):

- *Community Participant*—A school's main job is to prepare students to become effective heads of a household, members of a workforce, and contributors to a community. In school, students should learn skills their future employers find important, as well as practical skills they'll need in order to take care of themselves and others. Assessments should be objective measures of how well students can perform specific tasks, allowing teachers to review key skills and content efficiently or extend students' skills and knowledge.

- *Change Agent*—A school's main job is to help students capably work for social, political, and environmental justice. Students should learn critical thinking, creative problem solving, and communication skills so they can understand societal problems and work with others to solve them. Assessment tasks should have real-world relevance and should measure students' progress as individuals and within the group. Teachers should make sure that their students leave school equipped to be caring, empathetic, active, and informed citizens.
- *Marketplace Competitor*—A school's main job is to teach the knowledge, skills, and mindsets students will need to move forward with an advantage in the world. Teachers need to be experts in their disciplines so they can pass on the understandings and demonstrate the skills students will need to be successful. Assessments should allow teachers to recognize students with the greatest amount of knowledge and skill and to support those with the least. Teachers should make sure that their students leave school equipped to be top-performing members of society.
- *Curious Child*—Schools should be safe and supportive environments where students can ask questions, make mistakes, and be themselves. Young people are naturally curious and need active learning experiences that will stimulate their interests and challenge their intellects. When designing curriculum, teachers should start with the needs of the actual students in the room and make the material rigorous yet accessible and personally meaningful. Assessments are a way to measure each student's individual growth and determine what that person needs next in order to grow further.

Although many teachers think school should serve all four of these purposes, which do you think is the most important? When you're making curricular decisions, which of these four purposes is most likely to guide you? What are the benefits of this orientation? What are its limitations? Which orientation would you say some of your colleagues and supervisors have?

Instead of expecting conformity and compliance, let's assume and celebrate the fact that not everyone in a school will think the same things are important, and that diversity among teachers can be a source of creativity and strength. Teachers with different ideas about school's purpose can all contribute to a meaningful experience for students.

Clarify Decision-Making Processes

In *Understanding by Design* (2005), authors Grant Wiggins and Jay Mc-Tighe use the phrase "agreed-upon" a total of seven times (pp. 38, 58, 91, 92, 122, 143, and 318) to describe curricular objectives. Although agreement sounds wonderful, we might wonder *who* is doing the agreeing. Do teams decide by consensus? Do they vote? Do teachers submit proposals to an administrator or committee that makes the final decision? Do all educators have a voice in every conversation they care about, or are only some invited into the room? Are all voices fully heard, or do some count more than others? Is there a bias toward continuing past practices or adopting new ones?

Without opportunities to enact our values, articulating them can seem pointless—or even cruel, if teachers have made themselves vulnerable in the process. For values clarification to feel worthwhile, your department or team will need to know which curricular elements individuals have the autonomy to choose, which ones must be agreed upon, and who does the agreeing. Figure 2.1 (p. 21) contains a checklist to help everyone understand who makes which curricular decisions.

Create Structures for Safe and Inclusive Communication

Discussing values seems like it shouldn't be that complicated. If we want to know what matters to our colleagues, can't we just ask?

But communication isn't so simple. Perhaps you've been to a meeting where one teacher monopolizes the discussion, or two teachers debate while everyone else watches the tennis match, or someone keeps trying to assert her viewpoint but is always interrupted or shut down, or someone is so revered that no one ever disagrees with him. Or certain teachers never say anything, perhaps because they fear the group's judgment, or they don't think their colleagues deserve the fruits of their labor, or they've given up trying to make others understand where they're coming from, or they can't think of anything to contribute, or they're preoccupied, or they're just tired.

In order to encourage meaningful sharing, you need a structure for bold, generous, and smart communication. Bold communication doesn't mean everyone blurts out unfiltered thoughts; it means colleagues can voice their opinions without fearing for their jobs, relationships, or reputations. Generous communication means that people not only give their ideas but also overtly recognize each other's skills, passions, and needs. Smart communication

	Individuals decide on their own (perhaps after consulting with others)	Team members decide together by consensus or vote	Leaders decide (perhaps after hearing from team members)
Outcomes Conceptual understandings			
Knowledge of specific facts and terms			
Discipline-specific skills			
Cross-disciplinary skills			
Tasks Instructional tasks			
Major assessment tasks			
Skill and knowledge checks			
Special events (e.g. trips, speakers)			
Resources Core texts			
Handouts			
Work exemplars			
Tools (e.g. digital, art)			
Organization Title of unit			
Order of topics			
Length and pacing of unit			
Feedback system			

FIGURE 2.1
Making Curriculum Decisions

means that teachers get the time, space, and supports that help them do their best thinking.

The discussion protocols in this chapter—and throughout this book—help foster bold, generous, and smart communication, in part by *limiting* that communication. Group members might respond to certain questions individually and privately, so they can get their thinking out and then choose what to share. Discussions might take place in partnerships or small groups so that each person has more opportunities to contribute. Each person might get a set number of turns to share so that everyone participates equally. Prompts might be worded in a particular way to elicit deeper or more creative thinking. Rules might prevent certain kinds of communication, such as comments that reflect judgment or that could bias others before they form their own opinion.

Of course participants can decide to subvert the communication structures, such as by speaking out of turn, refusing to respond, or ignoring certain rules. A communication structure only works if people are willing to use it. That said, rather than rigidly adhering to any protocol, modify it so it leads to communication that matches your group's values.

Make the Process Itself the Only Outcome of Values Exploration

When we're pursuing a particular goal—such as designing a lesson—our attention tends to focus narrowly on achieving that goal (Gilbert, 2010). Also, when we feel threatened—such as when a colleague seems more capable, confident, or admired than we feel—our attention tends to focus solely on avoiding the source of threat (Wilson & DuFrene, 2009; Wilson & Murrell, 2004). But when we feel safe and contented, we become more open, flexible, and creative.

When colleagues don't have to focus their attention on achieving a goal or escaping a threat, they are free to focus on sharing their experiences, listening to one another, empathizing with each other's struggles, and connecting authentically. That's why the group protocols in this chapter intentionally do *not* lead to a curricular product such as a lesson or assignment. Instead, they focus on helping teams explore their shared values and respect their differences.

TOOLS FOR DISCOVERING YOUR TEAM'S SHARED VALUES

This chapter's exercises help pairs or groups of teachers clarify shared values. In *Learning Timeline*, you and a partner identify significant moments in your lives as learners, notice how these moments impact the values you bring to your teaching, and discover how your values might be similar even if your experiences weren't. In *Assignment Analysis*, your group looks at assignments that none of you created—not because you'll use these assignments in your course, but as a way to notice how other teachers bring their values to their assignments and choose values your group wants to bring to assignments you create together. In *Venn Values*, you and a partner share your own assignments or lessons with each other, but the goal is not to determine which is better or to find some compromise. Instead, discussing your practices helps you and your colleague discover values you share and can bring to future lessons or assignments you create together.

If you don't have the sort of relationship with your colleagues that allows you to ask them to do this sort of work together, try asking your department chair, dean, or principal to lead your group through one of these exercises during a meeting or as part of a professional development day.

Learning Timeline

Even if teachers have worked together for many years, they might not know each other as *learners*. This exercise allows partners to get to know each other as learners before working together to design learning experiences for their students. Partners share significant learning moments, identify one another's learning values, and discuss how they can bring their learning values to their teaching.

Partner Protocol

1. Individually, list some significant moments in your life as a learner. The questions below might help you recall significant moments. Some questions might lead you to think of several moments. For other questions, you might not think of any moments at all. Your goal is to come up with a list of significant moments, not to answer every question.
   - What were some important learning experiences in school?
   - What were some important learning experiences in your out-of-school life?
   - Who were some of your greatest teachers and mentors? What did you learn from them?
   - Which peers or colleagues have taught you? What did you learn from them?

- When did you struggle to learn something?
- When did you have fun while learning?
- What did you learn earlier than most?
- What did you learn later than most?
- What did you learn at home?
- When have you learned from being out of your element—in a new place, with new people, or from new perspectives?
- What were some times when you learned to relate better to others?
- What were some times when you learned to relate better to yourself?

2. Individually, identify five of your most important learning moments, and write each one on its own sticky note. Put the sticky notes in roughly chronological order so that they form a timeline of your significant learning moments.
3. Share your timeline with a partner, and listen as your partner shares their timeline with you.
4. Say back to your partner what *meaningful learning* seems to look like for them.
5. Together with your partner, describe some of the important differences between your learning experiences.
6. Together with your partner, describe how your meaningful learning experiences reveal similarities between you—even if the experiences themselves are different.

Reflection Questions
- What did you learn about your partner?
- What did you learn about yourself?
- What kinds of learning moments do you want to create for your students?
- How can you bring your learner self to your classroom?
- How can you bring your learner self to your relationships with colleagues?

Extension

This exercise does not explicitly ask you to state your values. Instead, it asks you to share some moments when your values might have been at stake and notice what you and your partner have in common. Although you and your partner had different experiences, you might find them significant for similar reasons, which suggests your shared values. If you'd like to state those shared values more explicitly, you and your partner can look at the list of values in appendix A (p. 187) and identify some that you share, based on the discussion you just had.

Assignment Analysis

During this exercise, your department or team explores how other teachers' assignments reflect their values so that you can begin a discussion of the values you want to bring to the assignments you create together. The Exploring Assignments chart (figure 2.2, p. 26) will help you keep track of your observations.

To prepare for this exercise, your group needs to collect four assignments that no one in your group created, so that no one in the room has a personal stake in the work. You might use assignments created by colleagues in other departments or grade levels, or assignments you find online. Look for assignments designed for your subject or grade level but that address content you don't teach. For example, if Jill, Vita, and Kenny were to do this exercise as a group of eighth-grade English teachers, they might look online for eighth-grade English assignments unrelated to books they teach, or they might ask their colleagues in the eighth-grade science department to share some of their assignments. When looking at assignments you wouldn't actually use, you can explore them without judging whether they'd work in your classroom.

The assignments you use don't necessarily have to be exemplars of best practice, because your group won't be evaluating their quality or deciding whether to adopt them. Rather, you'll think about how the assignments reflect the values of the teachers who created them and how you can serve your collective values when you create assignments. Instead of looking for what you consider *good* assignments, look for assignments that make you curious or that stand out in some way.

Group Protocol
1. Put out four different assignments that no one in the room created. If the assignments don't have titles—or if they all have similar titles—number them so that your group can easily distinguish and refer to each one.
2. Hand out copies of the Exploring Assignments chart (figure 2.2, p. 26). Individual teachers look at the assignments and fill out their charts. Although you might like certain assignments better than others, try to avoid expressing these preferences at this stage so that you don't bias your colleagues

	Assignment:	Assignment:	Assignment:	Assignment:
What choices did this teacher make that you're curious about?				
What skills and knowledge does this teacher want students to bring to this work?				
What seems important to this teacher?				

FIGURE 2.2
Exploring Assignments

toward or against certain assignments. For now, try to see each assignment on its own terms and focus on the values that guided decisions about how to make it.

3. Looking only at the bottom row of their charts, group members circle anything that they, as individuals, think is important. You might have to adjust some of your wording so that it still applies to the teacher who created the assignment but also applies to you.

4. Each member of the group takes a turn sharing what they circled. Group members take notes on what seems important to each person.

5. The group discusses anything that came up repeatedly as they shared: "What seems important to us?"

Reflection Questions

- To what extent do you share the values you saw expressed in the assignments you looked at today?

- To what extent do you share the values you heard expressed by your team or department today?

- What, if anything, did you see in other teachers' assignments that you want to try doing in yours?

- What, if anything, did you see that is not so effective, and that you therefore want to avoid doing when you create assignments?

Extension

When looking at the assignments, many teachers will get ideas for making their own. In fact, you might find it difficult to prevent teachers from saying which aspects of the assignments they want to emulate and which ones they most certainly would not. After finishing the protocol, group members could share what they saw that they might want to try, and what, if anything, they saw that they wouldn't want to do.

Some teachers will be inspired by the assignment itself. For example, Jill might get so excited about a geometry game assignment that she decides to have her students create games to teach about poetic devices. However, Kenny thinks it's more important for his students to analyze how authors use poetic devices then to create games about them, and Vita thinks her students should be using poetic devices in their own writing.

Other teachers will be inspired by a stylistic choice. Maybe the math teacher who made the geometry game assignment included a labeled diagram of a board game to remind her students of its key features, and both Kenny and Vita think students would complete their assignments more effectively if assignment sheets included labeled diagrams. Maybe Jill doesn't think it's necessary, but because she is listening to Kenny and Vita discuss it, she'll be more likely to ask later whether they think it had an impact.

Also, Kenny and Vita might not have much in common as teachers, but now they've discovered a practice they both want to try that serves their shared values. In the future, they can build on even this small connection. Looking at assignments together provides a great opportunity for conversation about what you're working on, what you want to do next, and what values are guiding those choices.

Venn Values

In this exercise, two teachers describe their ideas for teaching upcoming content—not so they can agree on how they'll both teach it, but rather so they can listen for how their different lessons or assignments reveal similarities in their values. For example, as two eighth-grade English teachers, Vita and Kenny could describe their ideas about how to teach *Bread Givers*. If you work with more than one colleague who teaches the same curriculum (like Jill, Vita, and Kenny), you can either work as a trio or do this exercise multiple times in different pairings.

To prepare, make two copies of the Examples of Values list (appendix A, p. 187) and one copy of the Venn Values Organizer (figure 2.3, p. 29).

During the protocol, your partner will describe how they plan to teach upcoming content, and as you listen, you'll circle values your partner seems to hold. After your partner does the same for you, you'll work together to fill out a Venn diagram that shows your shared and unshared values.

As you fill out the diagram together, you can discuss whether you endorse the values your partner circled for you. For example, when Vita describes her media stereotypes project, Kenny might circle *awareness* as one of her values. Then, when it's time for them to fill out the diagram, Kenny explains that it sounds like Vita wants her students to be aware of different stereotypes. Vita says that although this would be a good outcome, it's more important to her that her students approach media messages *thoughtfully* and speak *coura-*

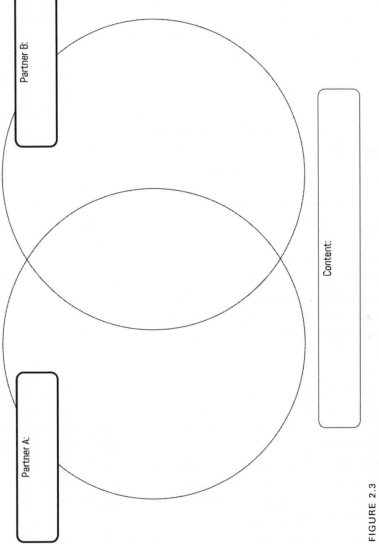

FIGURE 2.3
Venn Values Organizer

geously against stereotypes. If your partner identifies a value you don't hold, it's a great opportunity for you to clarify your values together.

Also, you might find more values you want to add to your diagram, beyond the ones that emerge from describing how you'll teach this particular content. Although you're free to add anything that feels important, you don't need to create exhaustive or final lists of your values. The diagram is meant to be a snapshot of your individual and shared values, with respect to a particular piece of curriculum, at a particular point in time. It's the beginning of a conversation, not the end.

Partner Protocol

1. Get together with a partner who teaches the same curriculum as you. Choose a partner A (who will speak first and then listen) and a partner B (who will listen first and then speak).
2. Partner A describes an idea about how to teach upcoming content. Partner B listens and takes notes. B can ask for clarification or more detail but should not express any judgment, positive or negative—including judgment phrased as a question such as "Do you think that will work?"
3. On one copy of the Examples of Values sheet (appendix A, p. 187), Partner B circles all of the values that partner A's idea reflects. At this time, B does not share with A.
4. Switch roles: Partner B describes an idea about how to teach the same content while partner A listens and takes notes. Partner A can ask for clarification or more detail but should not express judgment in any way.
5. On a separate copy of the Examples of Values sheet (appendix A, p. 187), Partner A circles all of the values that partner B's idea reflects.
6. A and B take turns sharing which values they circled and why.
7. A and B write the circled values in the Venn Values Organizer (figure 2.3, p. 29), based on whether one or both partners hold the values. If your partner circled a value that you don't endorse for yourself, your partner can still write it as an individual value, or you can leave it out of the diagram.

Reflection Questions

- Did any part of this exercise surprise you? For example, were you surprised by any of the values your partner identified for you? Were you surprised by any values you and your partner share or don't share?

- How important to you are the values listed in the middle, as compared to the values listed for just you?
- Describe how your partner's teaching idea serves your common values.
- What are more ways you can bring your values—shared and unshared—to your teaching?
- How can the two of you bring your shared values to your relationship?

Extension

After you and your partner have finished teaching the content you described during this protocol, come back together to share what you did. How did each of you bring your shared values to teaching this content, even if you used different lessons and assignments? What does each of you feel went well? What might each of you try next time? Even if you continue to teach this content in different ways, and even if you have different values, you can continue to discuss your work, learn from each other, and strengthen your relationship based on the values you share.

ONWARD

We've now seen various ways you can clarify your values, first as an individual teacher (chapter 1) and then as part of a group (this chapter). The next several chapters are about how you can bring those values to the units you design.

Use Values to Imagine Learning

Quinn teaches three sections of tenth-grade United States history and one senior elective on constitutional law. Teaching is a second career for him—he used to work as a civil rights attorney for a nonprofit organization—but at this point, he's been teaching for eight years. Quinn loves teaching his elective and often brings friends and former colleagues to speak to his class, and he also shares news stories and podcasts with his seniors.

As for his tenth graders, Quinn sees them as needy, struggling to understand basic concepts as if they've never studied history before. He guides them slowly and methodically through their textbook. Before each lesson, his students read and highlight a chapter section. Then, in class, he asks questions to make sure his students understand the fundamentals: who was involved, what happened, when and where it happened, and why. Sometimes he changes up how he goes over the events in the reading, such as by showing a video instead of asking questions, or by having his students compete in teams to see who can answer the most questions correctly. But often, he feels his students' comprehension is so weak that he has to spend the entire period going over the reading.

When his class reaches the end of a chapter, Quinn gives a test, always with the same format: ten true-or-false questions about historical figures or events, ten multiple-choice questions about a primary source document or map, ten fill-in-the-blank questions using historical terms, and three constructed-response questions in which students analyze causes, effects, or perspectives on an event. And each semester, the tenth graders write a five-page essay about a topic they studied that term.

Quinn's students do well enough on their tests and papers that he knows they're learning history. He figures he must be doing *something* right, because many of his students joke around with him before and after class, hang out in his office, and seek his advice when they have problems with friends or family members. Still, he feels like his class is boring and wishes his tenth graders had the same passion for United States history that his seniors do for constitutional law.

IMAGINING NEW POSSIBILITIES

Nothing is inherently wrong with teaching your curriculum in a traditional or familiar way. Maybe it works well for your students and for you. They participate in the activities and learn the content, everyone feels comfortable, and you've used the same practices for long enough to have gotten good at them. Teaching something new, or teaching your content in a new way, carries some risk. You don't know how it will go. Why mess with something that works? If it ain't broke, don't fix it.

If our current practices do everything we want them to do, then let's keep using them. But let's *not* keep doing what we do *only* because it's traditional or familiar. When people started to buy smartphones, it wasn't because flip phones were broken. People wanted phones that could do more. Of course, not everything a smartphone can do is healthy—psychologically, socially, or even physically—but only when we see our options can we select those that work best for us. We might have a perfectly serviceable curriculum, but we still can imagine new possibilities, and then we have the power to choose what works best for our students.

In imagining new possibilities for your curriculum, you might consider (1) *content*, or what students learn; (2) *tasks*, or what students do in order to learn; and (3) *resources*, or what students use to help them learn. Let's examine these elements further.

Reimagining Content: Connecting to Current Concerns

Teachers don't usually get to choose their course content. We have certain topics, processes, or works our students must master by the end of the year. Our course titles, such as *Geometry*, and even our job titles, such as *Spanish*

Teacher, specify the content we teach. But having to teach certain content doesn't mean we have to limit ourselves to it—especially when something important happens that demands a classroom response.

After the white supremacist terror attack in Charlottesville during the summer of 2017, many teachers felt moved to act. They tweeted with the #CharlottesvilleCurriculum hashtag and shared resource lists, knowing that white supremacist thinking and action thrive when we remain complacent, and that continuing to teach the same stuff the same way would only lead to the same results. It seemed like a moment of renewed commitment to racial justice in education. Once the school year started, though, did teachers use the Charlottesville curriculum resources or otherwise include racial justice in their units, or did they go back to covering their prescribed content?

The water crisis in Flint, riots in Ferguson, and school shooting in Parkland—and the activism that followed each event—led to similar moments when teachers asked themselves how to respond. Each time, some teachers set aside the curriculum because the event felt too important not to discuss, and others felt they couldn't set aside the curriculum because their job was to teach science or art or math, not current events.

We don't have to choose between teaching the material we're expected to teach, or teaching material that matters to our students, to us, in our communities, and in the world. Instead, we can imagine ways to connect our units to important ideas beyond our discipline.

To help students connect current issues to our content, we can ask questions such as the following:

- *What would a book character, historical actor, scientist, or artist we're studying say about this?* Students could write the article or research proposal this person would have written, dramatize the speech or interview they'd have given, create the artwork they'd have made, or simply discuss how the person might have reacted.
- *How is this issue connected to an event, time period, problem, or phenomenon we're studying?* What larger concepts or patterns are both the current issue and your current unit connected to? How can the two sets of ideas inform each other?
- *How could practicing a skill we're currently learning help us take action to improve this situation?* Maybe the skills themselves directly apply: the speaking

skills students learn in an English class could help them protest against human trafficking. But even if the skills themselves don't relate to the issue in an obvious way, *practicing* those skills might help students develop the habits they'd need to work for positive change. For example, persisting at a difficult math problem could help students learn the persistence they'd need to call a senator who's silent on gun legislation. Playing soccer in physical education class could teach the teamwork required for planning a climate demonstration. We can help our students see their assignments as opportunities to develop competencies they'll need to take action on issues that matter to them.

Of course, you already have lots of content to teach, and you might rightly wonder how it's possible to add more. As you consider new content for your curriculum, don't think of it as *adding*. John Muir (1911/2004) famously said, "When we try to pick out anything by itself, we find it hitched to everything else in the Universe" (p. 87). Think of the unit design process as tugging at the material you already teach to discover how it's hitched to matters of importance in students' lives, community, and world.

Reimagining Tasks: Assigning Meaningful Work

Students can receive, review, and use knowledge in such a wide variety of ways. For example, Quinn usually has his students explore new material by reading their textbook, but sometimes he has them watch a video or listen to a story. He usually has his students review the material by asking questions and calling on those who raise their hands to give answers, but occasionally he asks questions using a game format. Alternatively, Quinn could have his students listen to a speaker, read a novel, perform a reenactment, design their own games, discuss ideas with a partner or small group, draw maps, write diary entries from a historical actor's point of view, visit a historical site, research events in the library, or make art.

Expanding your repertoire of instructional strategies will help you see new possible ways your students can interact with the material and each other. For example, many teachers use turn-and-talks, where students share answers to the teacher's questions with a partner instead of raising their hands to share answers with the whole class. Turn-and-talks allow all students to participate at the same time. But turn-and-talks have limitations. Some students might not be able to think of a response when faced with the pressure of sharing with a peer. The student who shares second might simply agree with the student who shares first. One partner might talk so much that the other doesn't get a chance to share in the allotted time. The teacher might not have a chance to hear from every pair, and thus students miss opportunities to share their best insights with the class, discover others who might think along similar lines, and have any misconceptions corrected. In addition, talking to a single peer as opposed to an entire class *might* make it more likely that the peer will listen and respond but doesn't guarantee it.

After asking a question, a teacher could ask her students to write a response, have a fishbowl discussion in which some students talk while others listen, or assume roles such as those of Democratic and Republican candidates. Students could draw or graph their ideas. They could ask their own questions instead of answering the teacher's. Any of these methods will change how students interact—not only with each other but also with the material itself. Whether they learn *better* from one method than another is a question of values, but they learn *differently* depending on the task.

When imagining new possible learning tasks for your students, you might find it helpful to distinguish between *receptive* tasks, in which students take in information, and *expressive* tasks, through which they create some sort of response. During a receptive learning task, students might take in information by reading (for example, an article or primary source document), watching (for example, a demonstration of how to kick a soccer ball or a video about seed germination), listening (for example, to a lecture, presentation, or song), or experiencing (for example, a boat trip or a simulation of colonial North American life).

Receptive learning tasks often involve an expressive component through which students record or share their learning. They might annotate a text, take notes during a presentation, answer questions, fill out a graphic organizer, or have mini-discussions in small groups or as a whole class. But primarily, they're receiving knowledge.

An expressive learning task invites students to use what they're learning to create a piece of work. Students might draw pictures, build models, write letters, conduct experiments, film documentaries, act out events, play games, invent games, or make something else that has them apply, extend, and construct their knowledge.

If course content matters enough that students need to learn it in the first place, then it likely also matters enough that students should *do* something meaningful with it. Imagine that as part of his history course, Quinn has his students learn about United States physical geography. Presumably, he wants them to do more than memorize the names of physical features like the mountain ranges, rivers, and plains. Even if his students are not particularly interested in United States physical geography—after all, if the material is new to them, they might not know it well enough to know how it might matter to them—Quinn can create a meaningful task for learning about it.

For example, if he wants his students to understand how physical geography affects people's lives, Quinn could have his students sculpt various landforms from play clay and then ask questions about how these landforms might lead to economic opportunities, cultural boundaries, and political conflicts. Then, he could have his students look at a United States map and ask similar questions. Students could write predictions on index cards about impacts of United States geography and post these on a map. Then, as students learn about various historical events, they can see if their predictions came true and make new predictions.

Some expressive learning tasks will involve making physical things, such as posters or models, and some will be events, such as debates or experiments. Some expressive learning tasks might involve simulation or roleplay, such as having students act out different types of atomic bonding or imagine they're fashion designers creating outfits for different book characters. In any of these cases, students engage with the material in a meaningful way.

Reimagining Resources: Drawing on All Relevant Knowledge

Any knowledge that meaningfully advances students' understanding, development, or work is valuable. That knowledge can come from traditional sources such as textbooks, and it can come from the students themselves, their families and neighborhoods, and those cultures and perspectives typically left out of your subject's narrative.

For example, in a chemistry unit on acids and bases, the students might learn as much from their school's maintenance and cafeteria workers as they would from their textbook. If physical education students investigate what beauty looks and feels like, students could interview women of color, lesbians, and elderly women in their families and communities to find out how they conceptualize beauty, health, and wellness.

Reimagining resources encourages teachers to engage in what Christine Sleeter (2005) calls "the process of retrieving subjugated knowledge" (p. 91), or studying the topic from the perspective of "a sociocultural group whose experiences, perspectives, and/or intellectual work relates to the big idea [of the unit] but is marginalized in it" (p. 91). Guided by your values, you can bring typically marginalized knowledge into the academic domain.

Beyond reconsidering which sources of knowledge count as relevant, you can *make* knowledge relevant by borrowing theoretical models or frameworks from other disciplines to help students make sense of the information they learn in your class.

Imagine, for example, that Quinn reads an article about symbiosis, which is a long-term pattern of interaction between species. He learns that in mutualist relationships, the two organisms help each other, such as how bees get nectar from flowers and the flowers are pollinated in the process. In commensal relationships, one organism helps the other but is basically unaffected—barnacles have a safe home and a steady stream of food when they attach to whales, who get nothing in return but aren't harmed either. In parasitic relationships, one organism benefits while the other is harmed—a flea gets nutrients from a dog's blood and makes the dog sick. In teaching about the events leading up to the American Revolution, Quinn asks his students to characterize relationships between various colonies, Indigenous nations, and European nations as mutual, commensal, or parasitic.

Other examples of frameworks include the food pyramid, the periodic table of elements, Maslow's (1943) hierarchy of needs, and the new diagram of sex and gender (Bryan, 2012). What would a food pyramid of poetic devices look like? What about a periodic table of physical exercises? How would you describe the needs of an ecosystem using Maslow's hierarchy? How do the four spectra of sex and gender—biological sex, gender identity, gender expression, and sexual orientation—help us understand characters in a play?

A theoretical framework attunes students to aspects of the content they might not notice otherwise. Even if the framework doesn't directly apply to the situation your class is studying, it can serve as a useful metaphor, which "allows the efficient development of entirely new ways of thinking, while providing the guidance or a model drawn from a more known domain" (Stewart, Barnes-Holmes, Hayes, & Lipkens, 2001, p. 86). Frameworks offer ways for students to categorize knowledge, notice missing pieces, communicate about complex issues, and develop new ideas. Using a framework also teaches students that they *can* draw from other disciplines to focus their attention and organize their understanding.

It's hard to look for theoretical frameworks or models to borrow from other disciplines because these will be outside our realm of expertise. The best we can do is expose ourselves to lots of different ideas—whether through reading, listening, taking courses, or living our daily lives—always keeping our eyes open for ways people make sense of the world and considering how we might bring those to our curriculum.

RECLAIMING THE ARTISTRY OF CURRICULUM DESIGN

We don't necessarily think of unit planning as an act of creativity—at least, not one that's on the same level as sculpture or choreography. If we have to fill out forms that we hand in to administrators, or stake our jobs on whether we write learning objectives on the board, unit planning feels more like doing chores than making art. But there can be a sort of artistry in curriculum design. It is, after all, *design*.

Artist Laurie Miller Hornik creates whimsical mixed-media collages, with subjects ranging from dogs reading fairy tales to forests made of clocks to penguins invading her bedroom. She doesn't actively think about her art all of the time, but it's always in the back of her mind, so *anything* she comes across might serve as a potential subject. Her walks through New York City, conversations with friends, audiobooks, and battles against the squirrels invading her attic give her ideas she brings to her work. She also spends lots of time mucking about with yarn and paint and paper, discovering what she might do with these materials. Few of these activities look like making a collage, but they're integral parts of her process.

Laurie is also a gifted English teacher, and she sees designing curriculum as a process similar to that of creating a collage. Instead of playing with art supplies, she plays with her course content: books and poems, imagery and symbolism, prompts and rubrics. And just as any aspect of her life experience might give her an idea for a collage—not because she's actively searching for ideas but because her art is always in the back of her mind—her experiences within and beyond school give her ideas she can bring to her curriculum. But she doesn't throw in everything she happens to like, any more than she throws every finding into a collage. Guided by her values, Laurie makes thoughtful decisions about what to put into her artwork and her course.

This back-and-forth between generative and evaluative thinking—between playing with ideas and choosing the ones that work—is central to any artistic endeavor, including curriculum design. When we reimagine our units, we think like the artists we are.

Creating a unit thus can begin the same way as creating anything else, as an exploratory process, akin to collecting paper that might later be made into a collage, or to shooting lots of footage that might later be used in a documentary film. Try to find or produce lots of material—more than you'll end up using in the finished unit. As in filmmaking and collaging, you'll need to be selective and critical later, choosing the bits that will work best and structuring them in a coherent way.

Unit design involves lots of research: reviewing standards and curriculum guides, gathering print and visual texts, finding local field trip opportunities and experts (including the students themselves and their families), and collecting ideas for activities.

Sometimes, the materials you find won't be quite right for your students. A first-grade teacher planning a bird study might find technical guidebooks written for a much more sophisticated reader and simple picture books that lack the details he wants his students to learn. A middle school history teacher looking for films about the Vietnam war might find them all too graphic or too long to use in class. You might be able to adapt these sorts of materials for your students, or use them as resources as you make original materials.

The research you do in the early stages of unit design can be accidental: an article or picture in your social media feed, a show or commercial on television, a conversation with a friend, or an outing with your family will give you an idea for a lesson. As an exercise, try skimming a general-interest website while asking yourself for each posting *How could this connect to my current unit?* Again, the point of finding all of this material is not to use it indiscriminately, any more than a collage artist would glue every found object onto a canvas and call it art. Rather, the point is to play with new ideas, so that you can choose what to include based on your values—as opposed to only using familiar, comfortable, or mandated resources.

TOOLS FOR USING VALUES TO IMAGINE LEARNING

The three exercises that follow are just more ways to help you imagine possible content, tasks, and resources for your units. For *Resource Brainstorm*, you and a group of colleagues will help each other notice learning materials you might not have considered. In *Work What-Ifs*, you'll imagine how different learning tasks might shape your unit. Finally, *Curriculum Dice* has you consider your course content in terms of perspectives, issues, and concepts that don't connect to it in an obvious way. All three exercises are thought experiments and might not lead you to change your course. But you might get a few ideas to put into action. More important, you'll reclaim curriculum design as an act of creativity and think more flexibly about your units so that when new content, tasks, and resources do present themselves, you might see how you can use them.

Resource Brainstorm

This protocol draws upon the collective wisdom of a group so that all members get more ideas for their units. Each person writes down a topic, and everyone else suggests resources: people whose expertise would be useful during that unit, places students could go in order to learn, media students could read or view, and activities they could do. Figure 3.1 (p. 43) shows a completed brainstorm for a unit on Chesapeake Bay ecology.

If you work with a grade-level team, you could use this protocol at a team meeting, getting the added benefit of finding out what your students are learning about in their other classes. Or you could simply pull together a group of colleagues who are interested in learning from one another. Working with teachers of your subject means you benefit from their expertise, and working with teachers of many different subjects helps you think beyond the traditional scope of your discipline. You can use this protocol with any size group of teachers, but it works better in larger groups because you have a greater diversity of ideas, and teachers can choose which units they contribute to.

For this protocol, you need an index card for each participant. You also need sticky notes in four different colors, with enough that each participant gets three of each color. If you do this protocol in a room with no desks, you also need tape or tacks so that participants can post their index cards on the walls.

Group Protocol
1. Each teacher writes the topic of an upcoming unit on an index card. If you think your colleagues will need more information, such as a definition or very brief description, you can provide it right on the index card. The in-

PEOPLE   PLACES

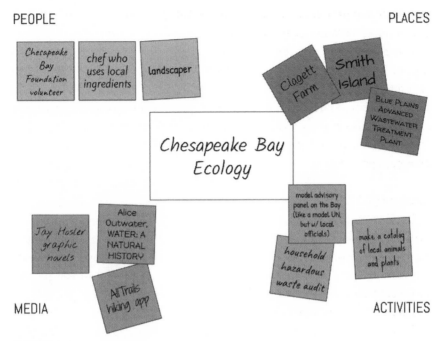

MEDIA   ACTIVITIES

FIGURE 3.1
Example Completed Resource Brainstorm

dex card's small size prevents you from saying too much and thus biasing or restricting your colleagues' suggestions.

2. Teachers place their index cards on desks or post them on the walls.
3. Everyone takes *three* sticky notes in each of *four* different colors, for a total of twelve sticky notes. Assign a color to each of the following four resource types.

   - *People*—Who could share their expertise on this topic with students? Consider experts of all kinds, including those in the students' families and communities.
   - *Places*—Where could the students go in order to study this topic? Consider places on school grounds or in the community. Try to think of places your students or their families visit regularly, or places that have cultural, historical, or environmental significance.
   - *Media*—What could students read or view as part of this unit? Consider all types of print and online texts, such as fiction and nonfiction books,

magazine articles, poems, data sets, works of art, advertisements, television shows, films, and videos.

- *Activities*—What activities could students do in order to learn this material? Consider experiential, reflective, and generative activities of all kinds.

4. Everyone walks around the room and reads each other's topics. Anyone who can think of a suggested resource for someone's unit writes the idea on a sticky note of the appropriate color and sticks it near that person's index card. Each unit topic gets exactly three suggested resources in each category, so once an index card has three sticky notes in a particular color, no one adds more in that color. Once a person has given away all twelve sticky notes, that person can help others who are still giving suggestions. If each person gives away twelve suggestions (i.e., three of each kind of resource), and everyone sticks to the limit of three suggestions in each category, then each person should receive twelve suggestions—three people, three places, three media resources, and three activities.

5. Once all of the sticky notes have been given away, teachers return to their own index cards and read the suggestions they got.

Reflection Questions

- Of all of the resources your colleagues suggested, which seems like it would most appeal to your students? Beyond that appeal, how would this resource be a worthwhile addition to your unit?
- Of all of the resources your colleagues suggested, which is most different from what your students usually encounter in your class? Other than simply changing things up, how would this resource be a worthwhile addition to your unit?
- Of all of the resources your colleagues suggested, which seems like it would be the most useful for students to explore when learning about this topic? Useful for what? Based on what you consider to be a *useful* resource, what can you learn about your values?
- Of all of the resources you suggested to your colleagues, which do you most hope the colleague will use? Why? Regardless of whether the colleague uses it, what can you learn about your values from the fact that you hope your colleague uses the resource? How can you bring these values to your own units?

Extension

After a month or so, you and your colleagues can meet again to discuss whether and how you used the suggestions you got. For those who tried using a suggested resource, what was it like? For those who didn't, what got in the way? Are there members of the group who didn't use any of the specific resources but for whom the suggestions led to new ways of thinking? Although it can feel gratifying to receive or give an actionable suggestion, don't measure the success of this protocol by how many suggestions people take. Instead, measure its success by the extent to which you and your colleagues begin to think more expansively about what a unit can include.

Work What-Ifs

If a unit topic matters, then you probably want your students to do more than just receive information about it; you want them to be able to do something meaningful with what they learn. Appendix B (p. 189–90) has examples of meaningful real-world work products students can create, using what they learn in your class.

For this exercise, you'll identify three different work products your students could create and imagine how you might include these assignments in your unit. The exercise proceeds from the assumption that we cannot evaluate how well something will work unless and until we've fully explored what it is and how we might use it. Still, the point is not so much for you to use the exact assignments you invent during this exercise—although you might end up doing just that—but rather to imagine new ways of teaching.

Individual Exercise

1. Write down the topic of an upcoming unit. On the chart in appendix B (p. 190), circle three different work products you could give your students as part of that unit. Choose from at least two different quadrants, and don't choose work products you already assign.
2. For your own reference, label your three circled work products *A*, *B*, and *C*.
3. Use some of the following questions to help you explore what assignment *A* is.
   - Where have I seen examples of this in the real world?
   - What about this makes me curious?
   - Which components or features stand out?
   - What about this connects to something my students care about?

- What about this connects to the mission of my school or professional community?

4. Use some of the following questions to help you describe what it would look like if your students were to create assignment *A* as part of studying the topic you identified in step 1.
   - If I were to ask my students to create this, what exactly would the assignment be?
   - How would I explain the task to my students?
   - If I wanted to show my students real-world examples of this, where would I find them?
   - What would their finished products look like?
   - What would my students' process of creating this entail?
   - What supplies would I need? How would I obtain them—or what version of this could my students create with supplies I already have in my classroom?
   - What would be a large-scale, long-term version of this? What version could my students complete in one class period?

5. Repeat steps 3 and 4 using work products *B* and *C*.

Reflection Questions

- Of the three work products you circled, which seems like it would be the most fun for your students to create? Other than it being fun, why would this assignment be a worthwhile addition to your unit?
- Of the three work products you circled, which seems like it would be the most useful for students to create as part of your unit? Useful for what? Based on what you consider to be a *useful* assignment, what can you learn about your values?
- Of the three work products you circled, which is most different from what you usually assign? Other than simply changing things up, how would this assignment be a worthwhile addition to your course?
- What would you need to learn in order to effectively teach your students how to create these work products? Why would this learning be worthwhile, regardless of whether you end up giving the assignments?

Variation

Instead of choosing three work products you think would work in your unit, choose three you think would *not* work but that intrigue you in some way. Then, describe what these three assignments would look like if you were obligated to give them. Don't expect to convince yourself to give the assignments. Instead, just see what happens when you push yourself to the limits of your creativity.

Curriculum Dice

Curriculum Dice is a playful way for you and a colleague to connect your course's content to other content that might be relevant. On dice, you'll write topics from your course and perspectives, issues, and concepts that *don't* appear in your curriculum. Then, you'll roll the dice to generate combinations of terms and imagine what the resulting units would entail.

The prospect of writing words on dice and using them to come up with ideas for curriculum might feel a little weird. Even the idea of cutting and folding paper to make dice might feel like a weird way to spend time. But the weirdness has a function: it unhooks us from traditional and academic ways of knowing and talking about our subjects, which frees us to use our imaginations, make unexpected connections, and ultimately discover ways to teach that we might not discover otherwise.

Figure 3.2 (p. 48) has the dice template for this activity, and figure 3.3 (p. 49) shows what the template might look like after a group of earth science teachers have filled it out. For the protocol, you need a copy of the dice template, a pen, scissors, and some glue or tape.

Group Protocol
1. Look at your copy of the Curriculum Dice Template (figure 3.2, p. 48). Notice that four shapes are on the page, made up of squares that will become the faces of your dice, and little tabs that will help hold the dice together.
2. Think of six roles that might give a person experience with the subject matter you teach, but who are not typically considered experts in your discipline. Consider professional, civic, and social roles. In particular, try to include at least some roles your students or their family members would identify with. Write these in the six squares of the shape labeled *Roles*.
3. Think of six issues of current importance. In particular, try to include issues that impact your students' lives, families, or community. Write these in the six squares of the shape labeled *Issues*.
4. Think of six broad concepts that interest your students, or have the potential to interest them, and seem worth exploring. These don't have to

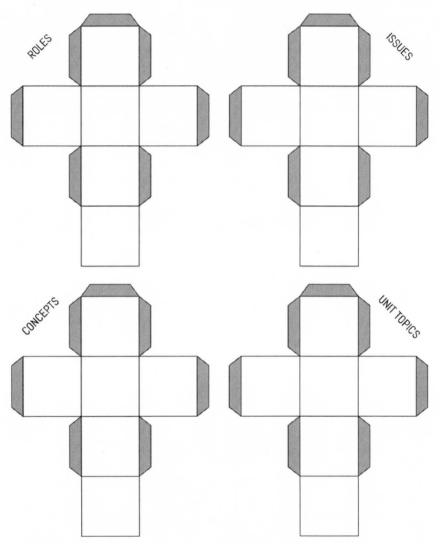

FIGURE 3.2
Curriculum Dice Template

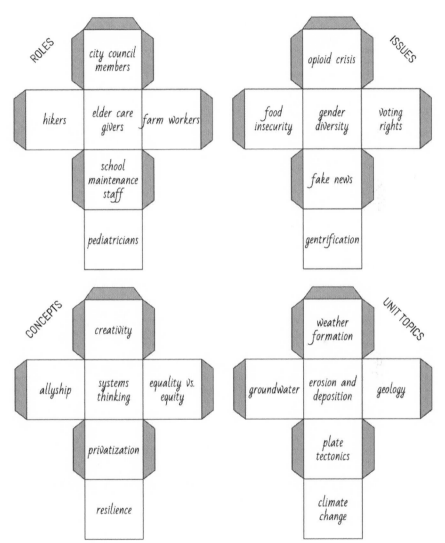

FIGURE 3.3
Sample Filled-Out Curriculum Dice Template

be concepts that come up in your curriculum or relate to your discipline. Write these in the six squares of the shape labeled *Concepts*.

5. Finally, think of six major topics your curriculum addresses. Write these in the six squares of the shape labeled *Unit Topics*.

6. Carefully cut out the four shapes. Fold inward along all of the lines, and glue or tape the trapezoidal tabs to the undersides of the squares to make cubes. You should now have four dice.

7. Roll all four dice. Use them to create the following unit titles. (You might have to add a word like *a* or *the* for the title to make sense.) Note that the unit topic will be the same in all three titles; it's the one that came up on the roll of your dice.
   - [Role] Perspectives on [Unit Topic]
   - [Unit Topic] and [Issue]
   - [Concept] in [Unit Topic]

8. As a group, describe what each of the resulting units would entail, using some of the following questions to guide you.
   - In a unit with this title, what content from your curriculum would you emphasize? What would you add? What, if anything, would you deemphasize or omit?
   - What kinds of learning experiences would you create for your students in a unit with this title? For example, would students have discussions? Ask research questions? Do experiments? Make art? Play games?
   - In a unit with this title, what books, articles, poems, datasets, images, and videos would you put into conversation with your traditional curricular materials? Who could come speak to your students, or where could they go on field trips in order to learn?
   - How would a unit with this title help students develop the skills associated with practitioners of your discipline? How would the unit help them develop academic skills? Relational skills? Personal interests? Career readiness? Adult readiness?

9. Repeat steps 7 and 8 if you like: roll the dice again, and describe the resulting units.

Reflection Questions
- Of all of the unit ideas you discussed, is there one you think you might pursue? What would be your first step?

- Based on your discussions, what seems important to you in your teaching? How can you bring these values to your curriculum, regardless of whether you use the ideas you generated today?
- Did anything come up on the dice that seemed too silly or problematic to consider? What does that tell you about the possibilities you *are* willing to consider?
- Did any terms *not* come up on the dice that you hoped would? What about those perspectives, issues, or concepts—or the prospect of connecting them to your curriculum—is important to you? How can you incorporate those values into your teaching?

Variations

You can play this game alone. Just make the dice yourself. After you roll the dice, journal about the resulting unit ideas, or even just think about them, instead of having a conversation.

You also can play this game with a colleague who doesn't teach the same subject as you. Make an extra copy of the *Unit Topics* shape. Fill out the *Roles*, *Issues*, and *Concepts* squares together but make separate *Unit Topics* dice using terms from your respective courses. When you create unit titles, you both will use the same role, issue, and concept, but a different unit topic. For example, a science teacher and an art teacher might come up with *Mental Health Provider Perspectives on the American Revolution* and *Mental Health Provider Perspectives on Kinetic Art*. You and your colleague then will describe to each other the resulting units. You might come up with cross-disciplinary connections, but even if you don't, you each will learn something about the other's curriculum, and you can support one another in considering new possibilities for your courses.

ONWARD

In this chapter, we explored why and how to think more expansively about your units. The next chapter is about how to focus your units so you can decide what to include and what to leave out.

4

Use Values to Focus Learning

Carlos tries to use a wide variety of teaching strategies to engage his ninth-grade science students. During his genetics unit, his students extract DNA from bananas, watch a film about genetically modified crops, act out protein synthesis, read a science fiction story about the ethics of genetic manipulation, play a game to learn how genes mutate, and discuss articles about new gene therapies.

Then, the students have a series of debates about genetic modification. As his students prepare their arguments, Carlos gets frustrated. He keeps having to tell them how the material they've seen in class supports or refutes their arguments. *They learned this,* he keeps telling himself. *Why won't they look in their notes? Why won't they just think? The answers are right in front of them!*

But although some students understand the science and can make connections between topics, their insights are more attributable to their preexisting knowledge and skills than anything else. Carlos realizes that many of his students are struggling. He wonders *If only some of my students are coming to meaningful insights, what's everyone else doing? If my students aren't reaching these deeper understandings, what am I doing? Can I even call myself a teacher if they're not learning?* He's being hard on himself: he gives interesting lessons and assignments, he clearly cares about his work, and everyone learned something about genetics. Carlos's problem is that although his lessons all relate to the same topic, they don't work together to lead to the results he wants.

THE UNITY OF A UNIT

A *unit* is a time-bound study of a particular topic: a week on Spanish vocabulary related to travel, a month on solving one-step algebraic equations, a trimester on West African empires. Units consist of learning tasks that help students understand the content better or differently than before and use their knowledge in a more effective or sophisticated way. Units also often include assessment tasks designed to make visible what students know and can do as a result of the unit. Finally, and perhaps most importantly, the tasks within a unit all work together to serve a clear purpose.

Researcher and educator Linda Booth Sweeney (2001) offers a helpful distinction between a system and a heap: a system is put together such that the whole has functions that a heap of its parts would lack. Imagine putting flour, sugar, butter, eggs, and lemons into a shopping cart. You have a heap of groceries. Now imagine that at home, you turn those ingredients into a lemon meringue pie. A lemon meringue pie has a function—maybe pleasing a crowd at the end of a summer meal—that the heap of ingredients wouldn't serve. A system works for a purpose. A heap's parts might have purposes on their own, but the heap itself does not.

An academic unit works as a system. It has functions that a heap of fun activities, or a heap of content that might show up on a standardized test, would lack. A unit meaningfully progresses from lesson to lesson, like episodes of a TV show or base-pairs in a DNA strand (both of which are systems). The unit functions as a whole to make deep, important, and lasting learning happen. Carlos designed a series of engaging activities that all related to the same topic, genetics, and that addressed various science standards. But his unit was a heap. Are your units systems or heaps?

WHY TEACHERS CREATE HEAPS

Grant Wiggins and Jay McTighe (2005) discuss what they call the "twin sins" (p. 3) of curriculum design: creating a heap of fun activities that involve similar topics, and moving students through a heap of content that might appear on a test. When the unit is a heap of activities, like Carlos's, the teacher introduces each experience, guides the students through it, and maintains order. When the unit is a heap of content, the teacher moves the class from a starting point to a destination, such as the end of a textbook.

Teachers who create heaps, whether of activities or content, might be complying with predefined expectations, such as having active students or covering certain material. If their own teachers presented them with heaps of activities or content, they might teach the same way, or they might rail against one approach that made them miserable by using the other. In any of these cases, the teacher puts tremendous effort into making their work look a certain way. Is your goal to make your work look a certain way, or is your goal to *teach*?

Teachers who create heaps often value making deep, meaningful, and lasting learning happen—even if they don't always succeed. (So let's not call their efforts *sins*.) Teachers might create heaps of content because they value getting a lot of knowledge into kids' heads, but does the heap effectively increase kids' knowledge in a deep, meaningful, or lasting way? Teachers might create heaps of activities because they value engaging and stimulating kids, but is engagement and stimulation an end in itself, or can it serve deep, meaningful, and lasting learning?

Instead of trying to conform to a predefined image of what teaching looks like, we can make deep, meaningful, lasting learning happen by turning the heap of content or activities into a purposeful, cohesive, focused unit: a system.

FROM HEAPS TO SYSTEMS

Heaps of content or activities don't transform themselves into systems, any more than a heap of ingredients will transform itself into a lemon meringue pie. In cooking, we have recipes that tell us which ingredients to use and in what quantities, and how to prepare and combine them in the right order, so they become the thing we want. But recipes only tell us how to replicate one specific dish, not how to create our own dishes. To do that, we need a set of organizing principles or guidelines.

Culinary author Michael Ruhlman (2009) explains that good cooks don't need recipes when they understand ingredient ratios and basic techniques, such as the ratio of three parts flour to two parts fat to one part liquid for pie crust, which cooks can flavor and fill however they like. Another pair of culinary authors, Karen Page and Andrew Dornenburg (2008), created lists of ingredients that taste good together, often in unexpected pairings. Aware of such guidelines, cooks can make delicious food without following a recipe.

Similarly, you can create units that work as meaningful systems when you use a set of principles or guidelines.

If a system has a purpose that a heap lacks, then in order to transform a heap of activities or content into a system, you need to figure out its purpose—what the unit will *do*. Aware of the unit's purpose, you can decide what to include in the unit and what to omit so that it serves its purpose. Let's look at three possible purposes a unit can serve: (1) inquiry, or exploring important ideas; (2) rehearsal, or practicing important skills; and (3) projects, or making important things.

INQUIRY-BASED UNITS: EXPLORING IMPORTANT IDEAS

One way to turn a heap of content and activities into a purposeful and cohesive unit is to create an inquiry. Students learn the content and do the activities as part of this inquiry. Let's say that Carlos wants his students to see DNA as a story. He could begin an inquiry-based unit with a question such as *How does DNA tell our stories?* The DNA extraction lab, the protein skits, and the mutation game would help students answer this question. After each activity, Carlos could re-ask the question and have students build their understanding of DNA as a story.

Once his students are solid on the basic concepts, Carlos could move into another question about the biology and ethics of genetic manipulation, such as *Should we change the stories written in DNA just because we can?* In considering this question, Carlos could have his students discuss various benefits and risks that come up in the articles about gene therapies, the film about genetically modified crops, and the science fiction story about human genetic manipulation. At the end of each discussion, Carlos could have his students revisit the question *Should we change our genetic traits just because we can?* That way, they'd continually deepen their understanding and be more prepared to debate specific instances of genetic manipulation at the end of the unit.

Using Essential Questions

How does DNA tell our stories? and *Should we change the stories written in DNA just because we can?* are examples of what Grant Wiggins and Jay McTighe (2005) call "essential questions." Wiggins and McTighe (2005) argue that questions are essential when they point to "core ideas and inquiries within a discipline" (p. 109) and help students "effectively inquire and make sense of important but complicated ideas, knowledge, and know-how" (p. 109).

What counts as "important" or "core" depends on values. Within any academic discipline, you'll find at least some consensus around what's important, but these are just statements of what people have said they value. When states adopt certain learning standards as "core," it means that people in power in these states share the values embedded in the standards. The term *essential questions* can be confusing because there is no natural or intrinsic essence of a subject, only the values people bring to that subject.

Essential or not, a question will focus a unit when it serves the following three functions.

1. Direct attention to what's most important about the content.

Instead of teaching *all* about a particular topic, decide *what* about it deserves students' sustained consideration throughout the unit—based on your values and the values of others within your school and professional communities. If the essential question asks about what matters, then it serves as a gatekeeper for content and activities: if they don't advance the inquiry, they don't belong in the unit.

2. Elicit higher-order thinking.

The revised Bloom's taxonomy (Krathwohl, 2002) distinguishes six levels of thinking: (1) retrieving knowledge, (2) determining meaning, (3) applying understandings to new situations, (4) analyzing how the parts of a thing relate to each other and to the whole, (5) making judgments based on evaluative criteria, and (6) creating original ideas. In inquiry-based units, students do more than recognize correct answers, recall basic information, and comprehend texts. They also apply, analyze, evaluate, and create.

For example, in an inquiry-based unit on genetics, students would do more than label a diagram of DNA, memorize the four base pairs, and correctly answer questions about protein synthesis. They'd also apply their understandings of mutations to play a game, analyze how DNA structures relate to their functions, judge whether a particular genetic modification is ethical, and create skits in which RNA molecules are protagonists that synthesize proteins.

During an inquiry-based unit, students might sometimes respond to the questions directly—for example, in a debate, class discussion, or essay. Other times, they might address the questions indirectly through an activity that helps them discover and deepen their thinking about the question.

3. Pique students' genuine curiosity.

When we hear a question, we usually are inclined at least to try to answer it, but if the question doesn't matter to us or sounds too difficult, we might give up. An essential question will elicit students' curiosity and feel worthy of their consideration if it relates to their lived experiences, challenges their beliefs, or addresses a real-world issue that matters to them. The question also should invite students to bring their own interests, stories, imaginations, and interpretations to the inquiry, thus making their work meaningful for them.

Writing Essential Questions

The following examples of questions might fulfill all three functions—directing attention to what matters, eliciting higher-order thinking, and piquing student interest—depending on the learning community's values as well as the students' interests and experiences.

- Persuasive Nonfiction—*How do writers convince their readers?*
- Order of Algebraic Operations—*How does the sequence affect the outcome?*
- Atomic Structure—*How does an atom's properties affect its behavior?*
- Spanish Introductions—*How can introductions reflect personalities and respect relationships?*
- The Constitution—*Why do we need checks and balances on government power?*
- Basketball—*How can I score when I shoot?*
- Winter Jazz Concert—*How can we control the way we sound, individually and together?*
- Self-Portraits—*How can color and shading choices become acts of self-representation?*

As an exercise, try searching online for essential questions on a topic you teach. Ask yourself what seems important to the teacher who created the question, whether the question would stimulate deep thinking and curiosity, and how it might focus a unit. Also look for questions that seem like they'd bore or confuse students, questions that seem too broad or too narrow to focus a unit, and questions that direct attention to knowledge and skills that could be helpful but don't suggest what *you* think matters most.

Many great examples—and helpful nonexamples—of essential questions are in Jay McTighe's book *Essential Questions: Opening Doors to Student Understanding* (2013). You might find a question that sounds right for your unit, or you might adjust its wording, or you might write your own question. Ultimately, whether your question sounds good matters less than whether it works to help you create a meaningful inquiry-based unit.

REHEARSAL-BASED UNITS: PRACTICING IMPORTANT SKILLS

Sometimes rather than exploring big ideas, students need to master a particular skill set through repetitive practice. For example, if students are learning to play the ukulele, find a logarithm, use lab equipment safely, or use semicolons correctly, they might spend *some* time discussing larger concepts (such as how semicolons change a sentence's tone, or who has access to lab equipment), but mostly they need to rehearse the skills themselves.

Although a rehearsal-based unit might sound repetitive and boring, anyone who masters any craft spends time rehearsing. Any performing artist rehearses, not only by practicing the piece from start to finish but also by repeatedly practicing certain parts, such as a difficult melodic phrase or a new dance combination. Any athlete understands the benefit of repetitive practice, whether of a single-leg takedown in wrestling, a free throw in basketball, or a jump serve in volleyball. And tradespeople practice: a culinary student might fry egg after egg to make sure the whites set and the yolks stay runny, and a carpentry student might practice cutting scrap wood many times before attempting to make a bookcase. In all of these situations, people are rehearsing skills in the service of some activity that matters to them.

In school, we ask students to practice skills they won't necessarily use for any activity they care about—at least, not in a way that's obvious or immediate. For example, math students might be asked to find the area of shape after shape, but many (if not most) students won't use this skill for a career or pursuit they care about. In fact, the only event many (if not most) of them are rehearsing for is a test.

What happens when rehearsal has no apparent meaningful purpose? Education professors Steve Graham and Dolores Perin (2007) found that grammar instruction isolated from writing actually makes students' writing *worse*.

Education professor Eugene Geist (2010) describes math classrooms when teachers overfocus on skill drills: "Instead of helping children develop fluency at computation and become more efficient at problem solving, these policies have produced students that rely more on rote memorization and have increased the level of anxiety in young children" (p. 25). Physical education professor Daryl Siedentop noticed a similar situation in sports units, which were "dominated by isolated skill drills . . . followed by poorly played games" where "less-skilled students were often overshadowed by more-skilled students who dominated play, and many students were left frustrated or just plain bored" (Siedentop, Hastie, & Van der Mars, 2004, p. 2). Out-of-context drills don't help students learn.

As an alternative to isolated skill drills, Siedentop developed Sport Education (Siedentop, Hastie, & Van der Mars, 2004), which aims "to educate students to be players in the fullest sense and to help them develop as competent, literate, and enthusiastic sportspersons" (p. 7). According to Siedentop and his colleagues (Siedentop, Hastie, & Van der Mars, 2004), a *competent* sportsperson "has sufficient skills to participate in games . . . and can execute strategies appropriate to the complexity of the activity" (p. 2), a *literate* sportsperson "understands and values the rules, rituals, and traditions of sports and can distinguish between good and bad practices in those activities" (p. 3), and an *enthusiastic* sportsperson "has come to value the experiences and enjoyment derived from participation" (p. 8).

As a science teacher, Carlos might have similar goals. He wants his students to be *competent* scientists who generate and test hypotheses, *literate* scientists who speak knowledgeably about various biology topics and refute poor arguments, and *enthusiastic* scientists who ask their own questions and do their own research, even after they finish his class and move on to the tenth grade. Perhaps you're aiming for your students to be competent, literate, and enthusiastic readers, or musicians, or Chinese speakers, or historians. Perhaps you also want your students to embody these roles in the fullest sense—that is, to develop the intellectual, relational, and physical habits of one who practices your discipline.

The key to a rehearsal-based unit is giving students something meaningful to rehearse *for*. Instead of practicing skills out of context—or only to do well on a test—students can rehearse for a performance that matters to them. They can develop competence, literacy, and enthusiasm along the way, and they can embody the discipline in a fuller sense.

Designing performances involves deciding whether students will rehearse for one big event or several smaller ones, and whether the performance will be authentic or a simulation. Let's explore these decisions further.

One Big Event versus Several Smaller Ones

Students can rehearse for a big performance, such as a culminating concert or poetry reading at the end of the semester. But another way to create a context for meaningful skill rehearsal is to cycle students through individualized instruction, cooperative practice, and low-stakes application. During Jeff Nurenberg and Tony Marro's basketball unit, each class period begins with individual practice of skills such as dribbling and shooting layups. The students then form teams, with student-coaches designing cooperative practice routines, such as having partners take turns shooting a layup and catching the ball. After these practices, student teams apply their skills in short games.

Learning any skill set will present opportunities to take on different roles, such as the writer and peer reviewer of an essay, the painter and critic of a portrait, or the speaker and listener of a target language. Giving each student opportunities to experience multiple roles helps them expand their skill set and gain a deeper sense of why those skills are important.

In the basketball unit, student roles include coach, equipment manager, and scorekeeper. Jeff and Tony's students rotate their roles regularly so that they all get to experience the game from different perspectives. The students also learn skills in organization, materials management, decision making, and leadership. To encourage students to support one another as they learn these skills, Jeff and Tony hold regular meetings with groups of students who have the same role; for example, they hold coaches' meetings so that students can share how their teams are doing and give each other tips for running more inclusive and rigorous practices. If students rehearse for many smaller events, they get opportunities to practice different skills and try on different roles.

Authentic Performances versus Simulations

An authentic performance has stakes. An audience views, reads, hears, or perhaps even participates in the work. The audience might simply be other classes, or the students' families and friends, but their presence changes what the performance means. Audience members could simply watch from their seats while students sing in a concert, deliver speeches, present an original film festival, put on a fashion show in Chinese, or otherwise perform. Alternatively, students could interact with the audience members in some way, such as by leading them through their class's geometry museum or on a nature tour of the neighborhood, or by posing as statues of historical figures that come alive when visitors speak to them.

Another way to give stakes to a performance is to make it a competition. As TV contest shows make clear, we can turn almost any skill into a competition, such as who can come up with the most creative simile that still makes sense, or who can solve the most division problems in one minute. Even if winners don't get prizes or points toward a higher grade, most people would rather win than lose, so competitions can be motivating. If students compete in teams, then they might feel a sense of obligation to their teammates even if they don't much care about winning. Of course, the corollary to feeling responsible to their teammates is feeling embarrassed if their actions cause their team to lose. Competitions are great opportunities for students to practice the sorts of compassionate and self-compassionate behaviors they'll need when they encounter life's inevitable wins and losses.

In contrast to an authentic performance, whether for an audience or in a competition, a simulation involves some element of fantasy and roleplay. Simulations allow students to use their skills in imaginary situations that they aren't ready or able to access in real life. For example, French students might imagine themselves in a Parisian café, enjoying snacks and having a conversation (in French, of course!). Environmental science students might play attendees at a national convention on climate change. Algebra students might pretend to be members of a city council reviewing budget proposals for transportation infrastructure upgrades. Simulations give students opportunities to use their skills *and* their imaginations within a temporary fantasy world that allows them to see how their skills matter in the real world.

PROJECT-BASED UNITS: MAKING IMPORTANT THINGS
A third way to create a focused and purposeful unit is to design a project. Projects are opportunities for students to learn skills and concepts *you* value through the process of creating work products *they* value. In an English class, for example, students might learn how to use precise language, vivid imagery, and poetic devices—skills their teacher values—while writing poems on a topic of personal importance, discovering their own ideas, and

developing a writer-voice. Projects also help students develop cross-disciplinary skills such as collaboration, creative problem solving, and resilience. During a project-based unit, all activities move students toward successfully completing the product, and students learn necessary content and skills along the way.

Calling work a *project* doesn't guarantee that students will learn important content and skills while doing it—or that they will find the work important. Engineer Sylvia Libow Martinez and educator Gary Stager (2013) lament that when teachers call an assignment a *project*, they often mean "any activity that is not worksheet-based or that takes longer than a 42-minute class period" (p. 58). A good test of whether work is a meaningful project or just time consuming is to see if this type of work product exists in the real world, or if the only time people make it is for school. For example, people write letters to congressional representatives, make budgets, and create websites as part of doing their jobs, caring for themselves, and helping their communities. But the only time people write five-paragraph essays, do math problem sets, or go on webquests is for school.

Projects give students opportunities to think critically and creatively about the material while bringing their interests, background knowledge, and skills to the process of making work product that is "substantial, shareable, and personally meaningful" (Martinez & Stager, 2013, p. 57). Put differently, the project involves creating work product that *matters*, to students personally and in the world.

Project Assignments as Unit Outlines

Art teacher Katie Moncton (2009) had her high school students study an installation by artist Robert Gober (1989), which included wallpaper that he made by juxtaposing images of a white man sleeping and a black man being lynched. Gober's work powerfully illustrates how in the United States, racism is as all-encompassing and as unacknowledged as wallpaper. Moncton had her students discuss the usual functions of wallpaper and then analyze Gober's. From there, the students selected two contrasting images from mainstream news media to turn into their own wallpaper. Moncton's assignment description might have said something like, *Using the work of Robert Gober as a model, choose two contrasting images from a mainstream news site, edit the*

*images to convey their most essential elements, and create a wallpaper sample
that juxtaposes these two images in a repeating pattern.*

A project description like this not only communicates the task to the students; it also gives the teacher a basic unit plan. Students will need to (1) examine and analyze Gober's work so they can use it as a model for their own, (2) discuss the concepts of contrast, juxtaposition, and repetition in art, (3) spend time looking on news sites, (4) learn how to edit the images, (5) critique each other's work so they can revise for maximum impact, and (6) create the wallpaper samples. Depending on how much time she has and her students' prior knowledge, Moncton could spend part of a class period, an entire period, or several periods guiding her students through any given step.

In writing an assignment description, you not only express your students' main tasks; you also imply yours. Whatever students need to do to complete the assignment successfully, you need to teach.

Teaching Cross-Disciplinary Skills

A good project requires knowledge and skills that relate to your subject area, and it probably also requires skills that relate to the task itself but not to your subject. For example, many teachers ask their students to make posters without teaching the basics of effective poster design. Teachers might ask students to make videos without teaching them how to operate the camera, check the sound and lighting, or edit the footage. Some teachers mention such elements ("No white space on your posters!" or "Make sure I can hear you on the video!") but leave it to the students to figure out what to do. Projects give you an opportunity to teach specific strategies about how to relate to others, communicate effectively, manage time and materials, and use technology—all in a meaningful context.

Sometimes, you might not realize how many skills and strategies a given project demands until after your students complete it and you're disappointed in their work. To become aware of every aspect of a project, try doing it yourself. Then, decide if you want to add lessons to your unit so you can teach specific strategies for completing each part of the work, modify the project so students don't need to do the parts you don't think are worth teaching about, or change the project entirely.

Let's say a Spanish teacher has the idea that her students could film demonstrations of how to cook traditional foods from Spanish-speaking countries. She thinks this project will be a great way for her students to learn food vocabulary and command-form verbs. But as she does the project herself, the teacher realizes that it involves quite a lot of skills—such as using a tripod and making an empanada—that she isn't willing to devote class time to teaching. After all, her job is to make sure her students learn Spanish.

Because this teacher wants her students to learn how to use food vocabulary and command-form verbs, she decides to have them demonstrate simpler food preparation tasks they already know how to do, such as making sandwiches, and do live demonstrations in class instead of making videos. As practice, she has her students watch professional cooking shows on mute and narrate them in Spanish. In these ways, the teacher keeps the project's focus on learning Spanish but still incorporates elements of her original idea.

APPROACHING UNIT FORMATS FLEXIBLY

As you start to imagine a unit for your class, you might wonder whether to call that unit an inquiry, a rehearsal, or a project. A dance unit seems rehearsal-based, because students are practicing for a performance, but if the point is to create an end product—the dance concert—then isn't the unit project-based? A unit on writing persuasive letters seems project-based, but isn't the point not so much to write the letter itself but to practice persuasive writing skills, and if so, isn't it a rehearsal-based unit? For that matter, can't we think of an inquiry as a sort of project? And shouldn't students explore important ideas, practice important skills, and make important things as part of *any* unit?

An inquiry-based unit focuses on exploring something (such as a concept, issue, phenomenon, era, or work), but students still learn skills—to help them discover, use, and communicate about that thing. For example, in an inquiry-based unit on the industrial age, students would learn essay-writing strategies to help them argue convincingly about whether so-called captains of industry such as John D. Rockefeller contributed to society in ultimately positive or negative ways. A rehearsal-based unit focuses on skills, but students still learn information (such as the names of different sculpting tools) that helps them describe what they're doing (such as choosing a particular tool). Students could create meaningful work product as part of either of these unit types. A project-based unit makes that work product the primary focus, and students gain understandings and skills along the way.

Figure 4.1 (p. 67) summarizes the three unit formats' goals and key features, gives examples, and shows the relationships between exploring ideas, learning skills, and making products in each format. But the three unit formats are not discrete entities; they're just ways to help us identify a meaningful purpose so that we can create a unit that achieves that purpose—working as a system and not a heap. Instead of trying to classify our units as one type or another, we can use the formats flexibly to help us pay attention to what's most important and decide what belongs in the unit and what doesn't.

OMITTING ACTIVITIES THAT DON'T ADVANCE YOUR PURPOSE

Sometimes, the biggest challenge in designing a focused unit is letting go of things we like. Imagine that a beloved assignment in an English class involves reinterpreting poems in different artistic media. Students make paintings, dances, and videos based on poems. One student bakes a cake with each layer a different color and flavor to represent a corresponding stanza of Edgar Allan Poe's "Annabel Lee" (2008/1849). Over the years, the teacher redesigns the unit as an inquiry, using the essential question *Which techniques do poets use, and how can I use them too?* The students learn to use literary devices purposefully in their own poems, but the art activity no longer fits. The teacher feels a little sad: no more Annabel Lee cakes. However, if the teacher values the creativity, artistry, individual choice, and multimodal expression students brought to the poetry-into-art assignment, she can serve those values in other ways, within the poetry unit and beyond.

If you feel reluctant to let something go, or sad when you do, it's helpful to notice and name these feelings. Emotions mean our values are at stake. When we feel sad, it means we've lost something we care about. What is that *something*? If you can articulate the values you're serving through the eliminated topic or activity, then you can reincorporate those values into your course in other ways.

TOOLS FOR USING VALUES TO FOCUS LEARNING

We've now seen three ways to turn a heap of content or activities into a system: through conducting an inquiry into an idea, rehearsing skills for a performance, or working on a project. The tools in this chapter will help you choose a focus for your unit based on what matters to you, so that it works as a meaningful system. In *Unit Title Generator*, you'll create different possible

	INQUIRY-Based Units	REHEARSAL-Based Units	PROJECT-Based Units
GOAL for Students	To explore important CONCEPTS that they didn't know about at all or use with as much sophistication	To be able to DO something important that they couldn't do at all, as skillfully, or with as high a degree of complexity	To successfully create an important PRODUCT and learn meaningful content and skills along the way
Key Features	Rich, high-level, personally and culturally relevant questions Opportunities for students to ask their own questions and respond through various modalities	Something meaningful to rehearse *for*, such as a performance event, game, or simulation Cycles of instruction, practice, and application	Guidelines that are open-ended enough that students can make the work personally meaningful but defined enough that they can meet expectations
Example Unit Titles	• Classical Mechanics • What *Lord of the Flies* Gets Right and Wrong • The Geometry of Circles • Surrealist Painting • Lessons from West African Empires • Racial Justice and the Water Cycle • Compassion in Young Adult Literature	• Graphing Functions in the Coordinate Plane • Caring for a Garden • Taking the Advanced Placement Exam • Playing Basketball • Navigating the City in Chinese • Choreographing a Dance • Modeling Exponential Growth and Decay	• Making a Budget for My Summer • Redesigning Our Classroom • Painting a Mural of the Industrial Age • Preparing a Healthy Meal • Building a Cell Model • Writing a One-Act Play • Making a Collage • Retelling a Myth
About the Titles	Feature a NOUN that names the concept, phenomenon, era, issue, or work under study	Feature a VERB that names what students are learning how to do	Include a NOUN naming the product and a VERB naming the process
Ideas & Information	Central focus of the unit	Help students describe and use the unit's skills	Help students describe the unit's product and the process of making it
Skills	Help students discover, use, and communicate about the unit's content	Central focus of the unit	Help students make the unit's product
Work Product	Develops and demonstrates understanding of the unit's content	Requires mastery of the unit's skills	Central focus of the unit

FIGURE 4.1
Unit Formats

titles and describe the units that would result, so that you can select a focus that works. *Finding What's Essential* uses perspective-taking questions to help you see the unit in different ways and ultimately articulate a focus based on your values. In *Unit Story Quilt*, you and a group of colleagues choose a focus for a shared unit by drawing what matters to you as individuals and looking for connections among the drawings.

Unit Title Generator

One way to notice possible ways to focus your unit is to imagine what you might call it. A history unit called *The Rise of Industry* suggests a different set of learning objectives and experiences than a unit called *Perspectives on the Industrial Revolution* or *Painting a Mural of the Industrial Age*, and all three suggest a more purposeful unit than *Industrialization*. The following list includes example titles for some of the units described in this chapter, and the Unit Formats chart in figure 4.1 (p. 67) includes even more examples of unit titles.

- DNA as Storyteller
- Playing Basketball on a Team
- More Than Wallpaper: Creating Art for Justice
- Spanish-Language Cooking Demos
- Techniques Poets Use

A unit title directs attention to what your students will consider or do throughout the unit. Inquiry-based unit titles, such as *Surrealist Painting* and *Lessons from West African Empires*, feature nouns that name what students will explore. Rehearsal-based unit titles feature a verb, such as *Graphing Functions in the Coordinate Plane* or *Navigating the City in Chinese*, indicating what students will learn how to do. Titles of project-based units, such as *Building a Cell Model*, include a noun that names the product and a verb that names the process.

Titles can pique students' curiosity—especially when they show how the unit will relate to their personal experiences (*Making a Budget for My Summer*), challenge them to try something new (*Writing a One-Act Play*), confront traditions or assumptions (*What* Lord of the Flies *Gets Right and Wrong*), or address a real-world issue that matters to them (*Racial Justice and the Water Cycle*).

Typically, we create units and then title them. This exercise, *Unit Title Generator*, reverses that process: you'll create titles for possible units in your course, imagine what those units would entail, and describe how they would serve your values. You won't necessarily generate the perfect unit this way, but you might think more expansively about what your units can include while also getting practice imagining units that work as systems instead of heaps.

For the exercise, you'll need a copy of the Title Terms graphic organizer (figure 4.2, below). You'll fill it out with verbs that name actions associated

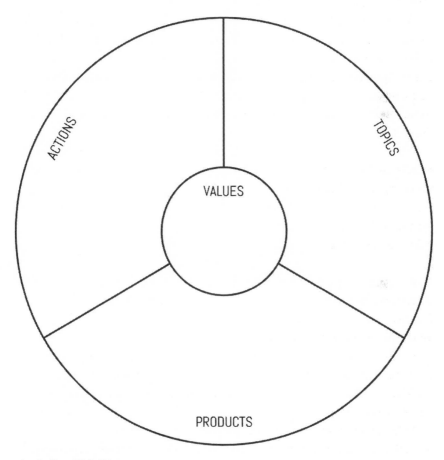

Inquiry-Based Unit Title:

Project-Based Unit Title:

Rehearsal-Based Unit Title:

FIGURE 4.2
Title Terms

with your discipline, nouns that name topics associated with your unit, and more nouns that name things your students could make as part of learning the unit content.

As a science teacher, Carlos might think of verbs he associates with the scientific method: *questioning*, *researching*, *hypothesizing*, *testing*, *observing*, *analyzing*, *concluding*, and *communicating*. For help coming up with verbs related to your subject, you can consult a set of standards or a curriculum guide, and you can also think of what real-world practitioners do.

When listing topics, Carlos could write the overall unit topic, *genetics*, and he could also write important subtopics such as *transcription*, *protein synthesis*, and *mutation*. As for work products, Carlos would most likely write *debate*, because that's the major assignment he gives his class already, but he might also imagine other assignments he could give. A history teacher might write several smaller work products she assigns, such as *timeline*, *map*, and *diary entry*.

Once you've listed actions, topics, and products, you'll use these terms to help you come up with possible titles for a unit, and you'll describe each unit. Then, you'll discuss how one of these units serves your values.

Individual Exercise

1. In the *Actions* section of the Title Terms graphic organizer (figure 4.2, p. 69), make a list of *–ing* verbs you associate with your discipline.

2. In the *Topics* section, list things you teach about during your unit. These will be nouns—people, places, ideas, phenomena, issues, eras, works of literature or art, and so on.

3. In the *Products* section, list things your students make—or could make—as part of this unit. You might choose products you associate with your discipline, and you might choose others that just seem like interesting ways for your students to think about the topics or practice the skills you listed. For help coming up with work products, take a look at the Types of Meaningful Work chart in appendix B (p. 190).

4. From the list in appendix A (p. 187), choose three or more values that feel important to you as you think about how your students learn, work, and interact. Write the values in the center of the circle.

5. Now, choose a verb from the *Actions* section and a noun from the *Topics* section. Write the resulting verb-noun combination at the bottom of

the page, where it says *Inquiry-Based Unit Title*. If the words you just wrote were the title of an inquiry-based unit, what questions would guide students' explorations? What kinds of activities would promote these explorations?

6. Next, start in the *Topics* section. Choose a noun, and then choose something from the *Products* list. Write the resulting noun-noun combination at the bottom of the page, where it says *Project-Based Unit Title*. If this were the title of a project-based unit, what would students make? What models would you show them? What would be the criteria for excellent work? What content and skills would you need to teach to ensure that students would meet these criteria?

7. Finally, start in the *Products* section. Choose a product, and then choose a verb from the *Actions* section. Write the resulting noun-verb combination at the bottom of the page, where it says *Rehearsal-Based Unit Title*. If this were the title of a rehearsal-based unit, what would students be rehearsing for? What would they do to rehearse?

8. Now that you've described three possible ways to focus your unit, choose the one that you think best serves the values you wrote in the center of your circle and explain how it does.

Reflection Questions

- During this exercise, did you feel excited at any point? What can that excitement tell you about what's important in your teaching?
- Did you feel frustrated or annoyed at any point during the exercise? What can that feeling tell you about what's important in your teaching?
- Are there tweaks you want to make to your unit's title? How will the title communicate what matters?
- How will your unit's title focus you, so you know what to include and what to leave out?

Variation

Try this exercise with colleagues. Choose actions, topics, and products together, but choose values individually. Invent the units together as a group, and then talk about how the units serve your individual values. Regardless of how you actually focus and title your unit, you'll practice focusing it in different ways. You'll also have a chance to discuss some of your values with your colleagues, giving you a starting point for later conversations about units you design together.

Finding What's Essential

Inquiry-based units are often the most difficult to focus. Unlike project- and rehearsal-based units that give you a specific outcome to work toward, inquiry-based units have no outcome beyond the process of inquiry itself. Essential questions shape that process by directing attention to what's most important about the content, eliciting higher-order thinking, and piquing students' genuine curiosity.

If you think writing a values-suggesting, thought-provoking, interest-piquing, unit-focusing question sounds difficult, you aren't alone. When Grant Wiggins and Jay McTighe (2005) were revising *Understanding by Design* for the second edition, they had to do "more painstaking back-and-forths of drafts of [their chapter on essential questions] than were necessary for any other part of the revision" because they "saw an inconsistency between the original account and widespread practice" (p. vii).

For this protocol, you and two supportive colleagues will help each other generate questions to use in your respective courses. You'll respond to prompts that help you articulate what matters about your unit topic, and you'll hand off the work of phrasing these ideas as essential questions to your colleagues. You'll return the favor by writing questions for them—giving all of you practice in writing essential questions and a chance to hear about one another's courses.

Group Protocol

1. Form a group of three—ideally such that each person teaches a different course and therefore has no stake in the units their two colleagues will describe.
2. Each person identifies a unit topic to talk about.
3. One member of the group (the "presenter") responds to some of the prompts below, filling in each blank with the unit topic they identified. The presenter doesn't have to go in any particular order or respond to all of the prompts. The other two group members listen silently and take notes.
   - Why do my students need to study ___ at this time in their lives, in this class?

- How would I teach ___ differently if it were for a different sort of class, such as a course in another subject or for an extracurricular program?
- What was dissatisfying the last time I taught ___, and what might lead to the opposite result?
- What conversations are other educators and practitioners of my discipline having about ___ right now?
- After studying ___, what do I want my students be able to do next?
- How did I learn about ___ when I was a student? What about those learning experiences do I want to carry forward, and what needs to be left behind?
- How does ___ connect to my students' other classes, out-of-school interests, or daily lives?
- How would I want my students to use what they learn about ___ to benefit their families, friends, communities, or world?

4. The presenter is silent while the group members say back what they heard, but framed as questions. Try to generate many different questions, or multiple versions of the same question. The presenter writes down the questions.
5. Repeat steps 3 and 4 so that each person gets a turn to be the presenter.
6. The group has a discussion about which questions seem to have the most potential for shaping each unit. At this point, any group member can offer suggestions for rewording the questions or ideas for teaching the unit.

Reflection Questions
- Did you discover anything interesting about your unit? Your course? Yourself?
- Which prompts did you find most helpful? Most challenging?
- What do you appreciate about each of the two colleagues you worked with?

Extension
If several small groups of teachers use this protocol simultaneously, then afterward everyone could look at each other's resulting questions, give each other feedback, and learn more about each other's curriculum and values. Ways to share include putting all of the questions into a shared document for everyone to comment on, posting the questions on the walls and having colleagues write comments on sticky notes, or simply having teachers read their questions out loud.

Unit Story Quilt

While the previous protocol has teachers help each other generate questions for their respective units, this one is for groups who teach the same unit. Teachers individually articulate what matters to them in the unit, find common ideas, and come up with a focus they can all stand behind.

During the protocol, you and your colleagues will draw images you associate with your unit topic. Whereas words can have vague or abstract meanings, drawings capture concrete and specific images that the group can collaboratively view, interpret, and assemble into a visual story.

To prepare for this protocol, you'll need enough sticky notes so that each participant will get six. You'll also need one dark-colored marker per person.

Group Protocol

1. Hand out materials: six sticky notes and a single marker per participant.
2. Each member of the group spends a few minutes silently drawing six images—one per sticky note—that they associate with their unit topic. If you can't think of six images, you can repeat ones you think are important. Keep your images simple. You can depict aspects of the content, resources or tools, students learning or working, or the work product they create. It's important to be silent and avoid showing your drawings to others while you're working so that they can think of their own ideas.
3. If you're concerned that your colleagues might not know what you've drawn, you can label your drawings or parts of them, but as much as possible, try to let the drawings speak for themselves.
4. Stick the images on a common surface, such as a wall or whiteboard, so everyone can see everyone's work. Discuss the images, using the following prompts to guide you, and filling in the blank with the unit topic.
   - Do we see any repeating images? How do these repeats indicate what matters to us about ___?
   - Which images stand out? How can these standouts help us reconsider what matters about ___?
   - What do the images tell us about the individuals who created them? What can we potentially learn from one another about ___?
   - What's *not* here? What *don't* we think is important about ___?

5. As a group, arrange the images into a quilt that tells a story. Deciding what it means to arrange images into a quilt that tells a story, and how you'll go about that process, is up to you and is part of this collaborative work.
6. Tell the story together.
7. Give the story a title.

Reflection Questions
- Is this an inquiry-, rehearsal-, or project-based unit?
- How does this story reflect your individual values?
- What can the story tell you about your group's values?
- What can the process of creating and telling this story tell you about your group?

Extension
Try using your story quilt as a way to introduce the unit to your students. If it's not practical to show the original quilt to your class, take a photo of it and hand out printed copies, or project it on a slide. Don't ask your students to guess what the unit is about, because that puts pressure on them to guess correctly and turns creative interpretations into wrong answers. Instead, tell your students that the images in the quilt represent ideas, actions, and things that will come up during the unit. Have your students write down anything they notice and any questions they have. You can then simply tell them what will happen in the unit, referring to the images in the quilt as you do. As the unit proceeds, the quilt can remind students of how the pieces fit together.

ONWARD
This chapter was about how to choose a focus for your unit, so that it functions as a system that leads to meaningful learning instead of being a heap of content or activities. In the next chapter, we'll see how to organize learning events so that the unit achieves its purpose.

5

Use Values to Organize Learning

Xiomara teaches seventh-grade math. For a unit on graphing functions, she wants her students to determine if there is a functional relationship, a correlation, or no relationship between two variables they find interesting. She thinks back to when she was her students' age and would stay up late to study but always feel tired at school. What relationship might she have found between hours of sleep and grades? She imagines all kinds of ways students could explore relationships between how they spend their money or time and how they feel emotionally or physically.

Xiomara plans to have her students formulate questions, collect data, make graphs, and present the graphs to their classmates. When she shares her idea with the school counselor, he suggests that the students could put the graph and a description of their findings on mini-posters to place strategically around the school, thus raising awareness about the issues they study.

Xiomara likes these ideas but wonders how to fit the project into her course. Typically, her lessons begin with a warm-up problem that helps students connect the previous day's material to new material they will learn that day. Volunteers share their problem-solving strategies and ask questions about the homework. Next, Xiomara transitions into teaching new content and then has students review the topic they just learned by reading about it in the textbook, taking notes, and solving example problems. That night, they do another problem set for homework, which they review the following day. Before a test, Xiomara schedules two review days during which she gives practice problems and confers with students who need help. If they need more support than she can provide during class, her students can see Xiomara during lunch or after school.

Xiomara worries that if she adds the graphing project, the unit will outlast her students' interest and take time away from other units. To make matters more complicated, she thought of this project while attending a math conference, where she also learned other activities she wants to incorporate into her units. She doesn't want the additional activities and project to feel separate from the lessons and problem sets her students already do; she wants all of the learning experiences to lead up to the project in a meaningful way. With these considerations in mind, Xiomara makes a unit calendar (figure 5.1, pp. 79–80).

Deciding how to focus your unit on what matters—whether by creating an inquiry-, rehearsal-, or project-based unit, or a hybrid of these—won't provide day-by-day blueprints for your teaching. You still need to figure out what your students will do, in what order, and for how long so that they reach the learning outcomes and have the learning experiences you value.

CREATING FOUNDATIONAL EXPERIENCES

Education and neuropsychology professor Tracey Tokuhama-Espinosa (2011) explains that people learn new ideas by linking them to familiar ones: "The brain receives information through the senses, and this information is constantly compared with what it already knows. . . . The brain then makes predictions about what it expects based on past experiences" (p. 212). At the beginning of any unit, students need opportunities to connect what they already know to what they're about to learn. To build a foundation for upcoming learning, you can have students recall previous experiences with the material, familiarize themselves with material they haven't seen before, or renew their curiosity about material they've seen many times.

Recalling Previous Experiences

One way to help students prepare to learn new material is to help them recall what they've learned about it already—whether in your class, other classes, previous years, or their out-of-school lives. Helping students access their knowledge might be as simple as asking a question such as "What did you learn last year about graphing?" If they look at their prior work from your

Day	Preparation	Instruction	Small Group Work	Individual Work
1	Brainstorm research questions about our lives.	How to choose a good research question How to collect data using surveys or interviews	Choose questions and create research plans where everyone has an equal role.	Begin collecting data for your graphing project.
2		How to plot points on the coordinate plane using ordered pairs	Play a battleship-style game on plotting points.	Do Problem Set 1: Plotting Points Continue data collection.
3	Homework review in groups	How to graph data sets in the coordinate plane	Solve problems on graphing data sets.	Do Problem Set 2: Graphing Data Sets Continue data collection.
4	Homework review in groups	How to determine whether a graph shows a correlation, a function, or neither; and whether a table shows a correlation, a function, or neither	Play a matching game to associate graphs, tables, and equations.	Do Problem Set 3: Determining Whether Tables and Graphs Show Correlations, Functions, or Neither Continue data collection.
5	Homework review in groups	How to describe functions verbally and algebraically in slope-intercept form	Do a problem set on writing formulas for functions and describing those functions verbally.	Do Problem Set 4: Describing Functions Continue data collection.
6	Homework review in groups		Choose problems for a review set.	Do the review problems that your group selected. Continue data collection.

FIGURE 5.1
Sample Unit Calendar

Day	Preparation	Instruction	Small Group Work	Individual Work
7	Analyze multiple exemplars of the mini-poster project.		Make tables, scatter plot graphs, best-fit lines, and equations in slope-intercept form.	As needed—determined by groups
8		How to speak clearly, concisely, and knowledgeably about a graph	Plan presentations.	Rehearse your part of your group's presentation.
9	Groups present their graphs to each other. Everyone leaves sticky notes on other groups' graphs to share observations, questions, and ideas.	Discussion: • Which graphs are correlations? Functions? Neither? • Why aren't most graphs functions? • What would need to be true for these to be functions? • How can we use these graphs to help us make decisions? • What other information would we want to know?	Turn the graph and description into a mini-poster.	Make a study guide for the test.
10	Groups use the previous day's comments and discussion to help them write a description of their findings.	How to make an eye-catching poster	Turn the graph and description into a mini-poster.	Complete the practice test.
11	Groups put up their mini-posters in strategic places around the school to raise awareness about the issues in the posters.	Review as needed after check-ins with each student	Study for the test.	Do problems in areas that need more practice.
12	Test: Graphing Functions in the Coordinate Plane		Reflection: • Write a thank-you note to each member of your workgroup that expresses appreciation for their specific contributions to the project. • Write a paragraph self-assessing your skills in math, research, and group membership.	

FIGURE 5.1
(continued)

class or another, you could ask questions to help them notice what they have and haven't yet learned.

If your students have never done what you'll be asking them to do, you can ask them to describe *functionally* similar experiences. For example, if students in an art class are about to learn how to paint portraits, they might begin with a discussion of different ways they depict themselves, whether in a memoir they wrote for English class or in selfies they took with their friends. Not only will students access knowledge they can then build upon, but you will get to see and assess what kinds of knowledge your students bring into the room, who might need support in order to access the material, and who's ready for more challenging work.

Becoming Familiar with New Material

Sometimes, your students will not have had prior experience with the unit content. In that case, you can provide a foundational experience that helps to familiarize them with a brand-new topic, process, or resource. Imagine that an eighth-grade history class is about to read the book *Carver: A Life in Poems* (Nelson, 2001), a biography of scientist George Washington Carver told entirely through poetry. This might be some students' first time reading a novel in verse, and it might be other students' first time reading poems as a way to learn history.

Before reading the book, students could flip through it and discuss their observations. What do they notice? How might reading this book be different from their previous reading experiences? What might be easier or harder? What are they curious about? Even if they aren't particularly interested in poetry, Carver, or history in general, how might reading this book be a worthwhile experience for them?

In classes where students will study material that feels remote—perhaps because it happened long ago or in a location they've never seen and are unlikely to visit, or because the concepts are so abstract that they haven't considered them, or because the task is so complex they can't picture doing it—you could have students experience a smaller, simpler version as a foundational task. That might mean giving them a less-complex version of a project, engaging them in an inquiry about a more familiar phenomenon before studying something less familiar, or practicing a basic process before attempting a more difficult one.

Elliott's seventh graders begin the year with an inquiry-based unit on basic geography, using the essential question "How does where you live influence how you live?" (McTighe & Wiggins, 2013, p. 5). For the unit's first lesson, Elliott asks a more specific version: *How does where you learn influence how you learn?* Some students examine a study room and conclude that the big tables are conducive to group work but make individual work difficult. Others observe and interview younger children on the playground to see how its structures promote different kinds of decision making. Elliott's students then have discussions and write reflections about ways location affects learning.

We might imagine alternative lessons, such as *How does where we eat influence how we eat?* or *How does where we socialize influence how we socialize?* Once students use familiar experiences to understand how their physical location affects their daily behaviors, they can begin to construct a larger idea of how physical geography impacts cultural life. Then, they can apply their understandings to less familiar situations in future units, such as how the Fertile Crescent influenced cultural development in Mesopotamia.

By beginning the geography inquiry with an exploration of the school, Elliott turns the students' shared environment into a topic worth studying and gives everyone an entry point into the unit. Bringing students' lives into the classroom at the beginning of a unit shows them up front that their experiences have academic value and that their new learning will be a meaningful expansion of what they already know.

Renewing Curiosity

Sometimes your students will have studied a certain topic or practiced a certain skill so many times that working on it *again* feels boring and pointless. Even if your students don't roll their eyes, groan, or sigh when they hear they'll be writing *another* lab report or studying *more* grammar, you sense that the prospect might not exactly excite them. For units such as these, a foundational experience can reinvigorate students' interest in topics, practices, or work they've done before.

One way to renew students' curiosity is to show them new ways the topic or process is relevant to their lives. Try starting with an experiential exercise or field trip, inviting in a speaker from the community, asking students to interview members of their families, or building on a school or neighborhood initiative.

Another way to renew students' curiosity is to create a challenge that has them discover the unit's purpose for themselves. Imagine that a teacher is about to start a unit on essays that focus on organization. He knows his students won't necessarily be excited to write yet another essay, so he wants to create a playful task that helps them see why organization matters. He finds examples of essays structured in different ways, cuts them up, and puts them into different envelopes. In groups, students reassemble the essays, discuss how they figured out each one's structure, and create diagrams to represent the structures visually. Having done that work, they better understand how writers organize essays and why organization matters, and they've become more curious about options for organizing their own essays.

Xiomara's unit on graphing functions also begins with an interest-activating challenge. Instead of starting with the math, she has her students brainstorm questions about possible functional relationships in their lives, such as *Does the amount of sleep we get relate to how we do on quizzes?*, *Does the amount of money we spend on clothes relate to how we feel about ourselves?*, and *Is there a relationship between the amount of time we spend with friends and how we feel?* Students have not only discovered the unit's relevance but also started their project, which involves choosing a research question, collecting data, and graphing the data to determine whether their behaviors and outcomes they care about have a functional relationship.

Consider your next unit. How can you connect the content to your students' prior experiences? If your students have not had experiences with the content, how can you familiarize them with it? If they're a little too familiar with it, how can you help them renew their curiosity?

SELECTING LEARNING TASKS

Once students have a foundation for learning, they're ready to explore new material. When you choose learning tasks for your students, consider the values you want them to bring to that task—*how* you want them to interact with the material and each other.

Choosing Receptive Learning Tasks

In a receptive learning task, students take in new information in some way, such as by doing any of the following activities:

- Collecting data (such as through a survey or direct experience)
- Conducting an experiment
- Examining an artifact
- Reading a written text (such as a novel, poem, play, timeline, article, research study, case study, data table, or essay)
- Viewing a visual text (such as a painting, photograph, diagram, chart, infographic, or comic)
- Viewing an audiovisual text (such as a film, animation, television show, or advertisement)
- Interviewing a participant, witness, or expert
- Hearing a lecture, story, or talk
- Watching a demonstration of a phenomenon, process, or strategy

Students might receive information while sitting at desks, taking notes so they can better remember and make sense of their learning. Alternatively, they might receive information by moving from station to station. For example, in an English class, students could read poems posted in different areas of the room and look for how each poet uses sound devices. In a history class, students could visit different tables to analyze the art, food, music, architecture, and fashion from the Roaring Twenties. In a physical education class, students could rotate through different areas of the field to watch dribbling, passing, and penalty kick demonstrations.

A particular receptive learning task will have different functions in different contexts. Think of a class looking at a photograph of a dancer. This learning task will have a different function for art students planning to take their own photos than for history students analyzing the image for clues about the time and place in which it was taken, math students looking for acute and obtuse angles in the dancer's body, or physical education students who will copy the dancer's pose.

Choosing Expressive Learning Tasks

In an expressive learning task, students in some way use the material they've just explored. In inquiry-based units, expressive learning tasks help students explore, apply, and analyze concepts so they can make meaning. These tasks might include any of the following:

- Annotating or talking back to a text
- Curating content (perhaps by making an outline, affinity map, photo album, anthology, or set of online links)
- Having a discussion as a whole class, in a small group, or with a partner
- Responding to writing-to-think prompts
- Playing a game
- Roleplaying a situation
- Debating an issue
- Representing knowledge in a written, artistic, or dramatic composition (such as a journal entry, cartoon, map, diagram, graph, model, collage, or tableau vivant)

Although some of these expressive tasks *could* take a long time, they don't have to. In an inquiry-based unit, you can assign quick, low-stakes tasks so that students can deepen their understanding or display their provisional thinking. Imagine, for example, that a U.S. history class is studying the Roaring Twenties, and they've just examined photographs depicting various aspects of daily life. The teacher now asks his students to choose one photo and write an analysis of how it indicates cultural attitudes of the time and whether those attitudes still permeate our culture. We can imagine students spending a week or more doing research and writing essays. But students could spend just a few minutes responding to the prompt, making observations and interpretations they can then bring to the next day's work—which might confirm their thinking, or might challenge or qualify it.

More generally, expressive learning tasks during an inquiry-based unit will require more than taking notes and answering fact-based questions. Instead, the tasks will elicit observations, interpretations, questions, connections to other disciplines, perspective-taking, storytelling, problem-solving, speculating, and imagining.

In a rehearsal-based unit, students might perform any of the same expressive learning tasks as in an inquiry-based unit but for a different purpose: to help them improve the performance they're rehearsing for. For example, students might have a quick discussion about what they noticed in a dribbling demonstration before practicing dribbling themselves, or they might list the steps in finding the area of a triangle before solving a set of geometry problems. In a rehearsal-based unit, students have two kinds of expressive learning tasks.

- Practicing discrete parts of a process (such as in a problem set or drill)
- Practicing a whole process (for example, in a scrimmage or dress rehearsal)

Because rehearsal-based units involve repetitive practice, consider ways to keep students engaged. One way to break the monotony is to have students practice different skills at different stations. During a soccer unit, students might practice dribbling, passing, and doing penalty kicks in different areas of the field; during an essay-writing unit, students might go to different tables to edit for spelling, come up with a title, and write acknowledgments. Another way to make practice more fun is to gamify it. Almost any set of problems or questions that can go on a worksheet also can go on a Jeopardy board, Monopoly cards (with teams answering questions correctly to buy the property), or Jenga blocks (with students answering the questions they pull from the tower).

Middle-school teacher Katie Powell (2019) invented "Worksheet Busters" that have students use physical worksheets in clever and playful ways. For one activity, students solve problems on worksheets, fold the worksheets into paper airplanes, fly them, pick up new airplanes, and solve the next problem. Powell's book and website have lots more ideas for how to make worksheet-based rehearsal more fun.

In a project-based unit, students' main expressive learning task is the project itself. They spend most of their time creating and refining their work product. However, they still need to learn *what* that work product entails and *how* to create it, and they might do other expressive learning tasks along the way. For example, they can make a prototype or beta version before attempting the real thing. If they're writing a play, they might first write a short dialogue between two familiar book characters, or adapt a short fairy tale for the stage, before attempting to write an original play. Other expressive learning tasks include:

- Generating material (such as through freewriting, 3-D printing, or having a jam session)
- Planning the organization or layout (such as in a sketch, outline, blueprint, or storyboard)

- Providing feedback to peers
- Revising
- Editing

After any learning task during any type of unit, students need to reflect on their learning. Content reflection includes noticing past knowledge, present understanding, and directions for future exploration: *What did you used to think? What stood out during the lesson? What do you understand now? What questions do you have? What do you want to learn next?* Process reflection means noticing past actions, present emotions, and future goals: *What did you do? What strategies did you use? How did these strategies work out for you? How do you feel about yourself as a result of your actions? What will you do next time?* Asking these sorts of questions helps students notice their learning and prepare for more learning.

Balancing Task Types

As you plan your unit, consider how you want to balance different kinds of learning tasks. New tasks keep students interested, whereas routines help students feel comfortable because they know what to expect and do, and they can focus on the material itself. Alone, students can pursue their own interests and develop their own ideas, whereas in partnerships or groups, they can generate ideas together and practice communicating. Working with the same people on multiple tasks allows students to connect more deeply and authentically, whereas working with different people allows them to see more perspectives.

You probably can think of other balances specific to your subject and grade level. What you consider the *right* balance depends on your values—as well as your students' characteristics and needs, your unit topic, your school's resources, and your time frame. When selecting any learning task, try asking yourself *How does this help students do meaningful work, form meaningful relationships, and build a meaningful life?*

SEQUENCING LEARNING TASKS

Instead of thinking of each day as a *lesson* with its own aim and activities, think of it as a *portion* of the larger unit. Just as each chapter in a novel or episode in a television series adds to the progression of the story, the learning tasks within a unit work together to advance students' understanding. As you select learning tasks for your students, consider how each leads to the next and how it contributes to the unit's larger purpose.

Inquiries Are Integrative

In inquiry-based units, students do activities that expand, complicate, or qualify how they understand the unit topic. Inquiries are *integrative*; that is, each learning task contributes to a larger understanding of the topic.

When sequencing an inquiry-based unit, you can take a parts-to-whole or a whole-to-parts approach. A parts-to-whole approach follows a series of events (such as the conflicts leading up to the Revolutionary War) or the development of an idea (such as the various discoveries leading to our current understanding of dinosaurs), ultimately leading to a fuller understanding of the topic. A whole-to-parts approach begins with a provisional definition or overview of the topic and proceeds through different components, features, or perspectives. For example, students might begin a geometry unit on circles by defining basic terms such as *circle* and *radius*, then explore various theorems about circles.

Any question about a topic inevitably will lead to more questions, and it's not always clear which question will serve as a good entry point, or where to go from there. One way to create a sequence is to write subsidiary questions of the unit's essential question, and then put these questions into an order such that each builds on the one before. When Elliott created his lesson on *How does where you learn influence how you learn?*, he simply substituted the more specific word *learn* for the general word *live* in the essential question, *How does where you live influence how you live?*—thus elegantly scaling down a unit-based question into something students could access in a single lesson while also preparing them for more abstract understandings later in the unit.

Subsidiary questions can serve the same purposes for individual lessons that essential questions serve for units: they direct attention to what matters, elicit deep thinking, and get your students interested. If you repeat words from question to question, or if your questions follow a pattern, you can help your students (and yourself) see how the lessons create a meaningful progression toward a larger understanding.

Figure 5.2 (p. 89) shows a series of lesson-focusing questions for a unit on how poetic devices work. First, students explore why poets write poetry, and then they discover how various poetic devices serve the poet's purpose. Notice that some of the words in a given question appear in the next question (such as the word *topic* in questions 2–4), and that sometimes a series of questions uses a pattern (such as the alternating *Why do poets* and *How can I* pattern in questions 5–12).

Notice, too, that each lesson's question serves as a subsidiary question of the unit's essential question *What techniques do poets use, and how can I use them too?* The teacher wouldn't necessarily pose these questions and have students respond. Instead, she might have students perform or illustrate poems, go on a poetry scavenger hunt to find examples of different devices, or use the devices while playing a game or writing original poetry. Through such activities, students arrive at their own responses to each focusing question.

FIGURE 5.2
Series of Lesson-Focusing Questions

If you sequence your inquiry using multiple perspectives on an event or issue, think critically about *which* perspectives you put first or give the most attention to, because students might conclude that these are the right or normal views. Let's take an example of one of the most painful and shameful moments in United States history: the Indian Removal Act, which Andrew Jackson signed into law in 1830, bringing about the theft of Indigenous land and the forced relocation of Indigenous peoples, amounting to genocide. If the teacher presented Indigenous perspectives *first*, then students would see these perspectives as central. If the teacher first taught about the lives of white American settlers, then the students might get the impression that their perspective matters most. Sequencing an inquiry isn't just putting topics into a logical order; it's an expression of values.

Rehearsals Are Cumulative

In rehearsal-based units, students repeatedly practice skills, add to their skill set, and undertake increasingly complex processes. Rehearsal-based units are *cumulative*; that is, students both use and build on previous learning as they go. Some educators use the word *spiraling* to describe this process, because students continually go back to the skills they've used before, practicing these as part of larger and more challenging tasks, and picking up more skills along the way—just as a snail shell spirals back toward the same points but also grows in size.

Imagine a unit in a percussion class, where students are rehearsing a medley of Prince songs for the winter concert. On the first day, they might learn the beginning of the medley, or they might start with the easiest song, or the most difficult one. Each day, they practice the part they learned the day before and then add to it until they've learned the entire medley. After that, they might rehearse the medley from start to finish, or they might repeatedly practice the most challenging sections.

When you sequence a rehearsal-based unit, you could move start-to-finish through a single work, whether a musical composition or a textbook. Alternatively, you could start with the easiest content and increase the level of challenge over time, or you could start with the most challenging content because students need the most time to practice it.

Neurologist-turned-teacher Judy Willis (2011) describes how in video games, each task has a clear objective (like getting past a baddie) and the game has an ultimate goal (like saving the city). Increasing scores, levels, and powers provide tangible evidence of progress. Willis (2011) explains that when students feel they're making progress toward a meaningful outcome, a rush of dopamine rewards their brains in two ways: it makes them feel pleasure, which is motivating; and it reinforces the neural pathway they used to achieve the progress, which helps them repeat successful behaviors. During a rehearsal-based unit, students not only need a meaningful goal; they need each learning task to represent progress toward that goal.

Projects Are Iterative

In a project-based unit, students create a piece of original work and get feedback that helps them improve it. That feedback might come from a variety of sources. You might have students test their creations—for example, by putting weight on a model bridge to test its load-bearing capacity, measuring the internal temperature of a cake to test its doneness, or reading an essay aloud to test whether its sentences make sense. You, as the teacher, might offer guidance, and you might have students form pairs or groups to make observations and ask questions about one another's work.

After getting feedback, students return to their creations to make adjustments. Thus, projects are *iterative*; students make their work products increasingly effective based on criteria for excellence. This iterative process includes four work phases: (1) *experiential*, when students encounter models of the type of work they'll create, or interview people whose needs their work will meet; (2) *reflective*, when students debrief the experience and discuss options for their own work; (3) *generative*, when students create their work products based on their discoveries; and (4) *evaluative*, when students notice how their work-in-progress matches up with criteria for success. At any point, students might return to any phase.

Imagine, for example, that students in a Spanish class are making annotated maps of the school for Spanish-speaking parents and guardians. Their experiential work includes looking at annotated maps of other buildings and attractions in their neighborhood, as well as interviewing their parents and guardians to find out what they'd want to know about the school. Reflective work includes sharing their findings in small groups and making decisions about what to put on their maps. Their generative work is to make the maps, and their evaluative work involves looking at other groups' in-progress maps to get ideas for what they could add or change in their own. From there, students might need to do more experiential, reflective, or generative work. When you sequence a project-based unit, include all four work stages as well as time for students to revisit each stage as needed.

REGULARLY RETURNING TO WHAT MATTERS

Even when you sequence learning tasks to build on each other toward a meaningful outcome, students still can forget the unit's larger purpose. For example, if Elliott hadn't framed his *How does where we learn affect how we learn?* lesson within the larger context of connecting physical and cultural geography, his students might have wondered why they had to run around campus taking notes about their school when the whole point of the course was to learn about *other* places.

Regularly returning to an inquiry's essential question, a process's ultimate goal, or a project's criteria helps students synthesize their understandings and prevents them from getting lost in details. Returning to what matters can be as simple as posting an essential question, process outline, or project rubric on the classroom wall and briefly explaining how each day's lesson connects to it. Students also can discuss, with classmates or through writing, how particular learning experiences serve the unit's overall purpose.

Returning to what matters can also mean helping students notice how their actions serve community values. Daryl Siedentop and his colleagues (2004) point out that learning a sport "creates the context within which students can learn valuable personal and social lessons" about mutual support, fair participation, and personal responsibility, but it's "up to the teacher and students, working together, to take advantage of the opportunities the context provides" (p. 93). If supportiveness is an important community value, then a teacher—of physical education or any subject—might have students rate each other's supportiveness, write reflections on how supportively they behaved toward their classmates, or identify things classmates did to support them. Reflecting on behaviors related to *any* value can help students retain those behaviors and use them within and beyond the class.

ALLOCATING TIME FOR A UNIT

Teachers typically must cover some predetermined amount of content in a year—whether that means having students read all of the books on a list, perform in scheduled concerts, write a certain number of essays per trimester, or master the skills articulated in state standards for their subject and grade level. But have you ever made or heard statements like these?

- "We didn't get to the water cycle this year."
- "I'd love to do more of that social emotional stuff, but I don't know where to fit it in."
- "My third-period class is way ahead of my fourth-period class."
- "How is your class already up to the subjunctive? You're so fast!"
- "We had so many snow days and special assemblies this year that we haven't gotten through the civil rights movement yet."
- "The graphing functions project felt rushed this year, but we had to finish it before winter break."

Many teachers feel they don't have enough time to teach their content. That's because there's no such thing as *enough* time for learning. Inquiries potentially could go on forever, because you can ask an almost unlimited number of questions about any given topic. Rehearsals also could go on forever; even students who achieve mastery could continue rehearsing to keep themselves sharp. (Just ask any singer, chef, or athlete when they expect to stop practicing.) And projects can go on forever, because students might come up with better versions of their cars, posters, or poems. (Just ask authors who have written second editions of their books!)

But just because we don't, won't, and can't have enough time for our content doesn't mean we should ignore the calendar. Determining an approximate length for your unit allows you to use your most precious resource—time—in a way that's consistent with your values.

Unit Length and Expectations

How much time we devote to a given unit both reflects and produces our expectations. Education author Ron Berger (2013) collects student work samples that he considers "exemplary—beautiful and accurate, representative of strong content knowledge and critical thinking skills." On his Models of Excellence website, Berger posts these professional-quality work samples, which include a first-grader's butterfly drawing that looks like it belongs in a published field guide, a second-grade class's book about snakes that also looks publishable, and a high-school group's energy audit that convinced their city's mayor to make money-saving upgrades to buildings.

Units that culminate in such high-quality work products take weeks or even months so that students have time for extensive research and observation, collaborative planning, and multiple rounds of feedback and revision. According to Berger, that time is worthwhile: "Once a student creates work of value for an authentic audience beyond the classroom—work that is sophisticated, accurate, important and beautiful—that student is never the same. When you have done quality work, deeper work, you know you are always capable of doing more" (Berger, 2013, n.p.).

Then again, maybe instead of a long unit, you want to leave time for *other* units that provide opportunities for students to explore different topics and experiment with new ways of thinking. Maybe you're concerned that a unit that lasts long enough for students to create professional-quality work products will outlast their curiosity, and class will become tedious. Maybe you teach students who, given time to keep working, will strive for perfection in a way that isn't helpful or healthy.

Because any learning experience could go on forever, but no unit will, we need to decide how much time we're willing to spend and set our expectations accordingly. That doesn't mean we're lowering our expectations *of the students*; it means we're helping them notice what they can realistically accomplish *within a particular time frame*—which is a skill in itself.

Xiomara could have made her graphing functions unit take more or less time, but she decided to portion her unit into twelve lessons (as shown in figure 5.1, pp. 79–80). That's enough time for her students to understand the concept of a functional relationship, practice writing and graphing functions, collect data about possible functional relationships in their lives, and display that data on posters—to the extent that's required by standards and that serves her values.

Planned Flexibility

Writing a unit calendar doesn't mean you now must stick to it. You might get better ideas for lessons. You might talk to a colleague about how a lesson just went, and they'll have an idea for what you can do next. Your students might express interest in a particular topic. Or they might express frustration and need more examples, strategy instruction, feedback, or work time. A relevant exhibit might open at an art museum. The author of the book your class has been reading might be accused of making up stories he'd claimed were true. A hurricane might force your school to close for a week. Your students might zip through the content in much less time than you'd expected.

With all that can happen, a unit calendar isn't limiting; it's helpful. The movie *Apollo 13* has a scene when the crew has to reenter the Earth's atmosphere at the proper angle, but they don't have enough power to turn on their navigation computer. The astronauts keep the Earth in the window to help them maintain their course. A unit plan serves this navigating function: it reminds you of decisions you've made based on your values, helps you decide whether your inevitable adjustments will keep your unit heading in a valued direction, and shows you how to course-correct when you stray.

To leave time for interruptions, difficulties, and detours, consider building a few extra days into each unit. If you teach multiple sections of the same course, building in a few extra days allows a group that needs a bit more time to complete an activity or learn a skill to catch up with a group that moves more quickly.

Xiomara has planned a twelve-lesson unit but blocks out fifteen class periods on her calendar, thus giving her three extra days in case her students need more practice, strategy instruction, or work time—or if they're curious about a topic and want to pursue it further. If her students end up not needing the days, they can take more time to share their projects with one another or reflect on their work process, or they can start the next unit. Just as an expansion joint allows a bridge to accommodate temperature changes, building extra days into your units helps you accommodate any emergent needs.

TOOLS FOR USING VALUES TO ORGANIZE LEARNING

This chapter identified questions to consider as you organize your unit into a series of learning experiences:

- What learning tasks will your students do?
- In what order will they do these tasks?
- How will you build in regular opportunities for students to revisit the unit's purpose?
- How many days will you devote to this unit?
- How much time will you spend on each learning task?

- How much time will you build in to accommodate interruptions, students' needs and interests, and teachable moments?

The tools that follow will help you assess whether you've organized your unit in a way that serves your values. In *Unit Write-Up*, you'll describe your unit in a brief paragraph to see if its scope and sequence make sense. *Quarters* helps you notice whether you've allotted time in a way that serves your values and explore alternative ways to allot time that might serve your values better. In *Grading Your Units*, you'll identify criteria for making a unit meaningful, and then according to those criteria, you'll grade how meaningful your unit is, as it's currently organized.

Unit Write-Up

One way to see how much sense something makes is to explain it to another person. During this protocol, *Unit Write-Up*, you'll write a short paragraph about your unit and read it to a colleague. Then, your colleague will say back to you what your unit entails. If they can do that, then you know you've organized your unit in a way that makes sense. Any mistakes could indicate places where you might need to articulate the unit's scope or sequence more clearly. Any changes your partner makes might indicate that the unit makes more sense to him the way they told it, so you might either revise your unit to match their explanation or more clearly articulate why you've organized it as you have.

Finally, your colleague will share what seems important to you in your unit, so that you can see what messages or meanings come across, decide whether these are the values you want to communicate, and adjust your unit as you see fit.

If your partner also is working on unit organization, then after working through this protocol you can switch roles and start over from the beginning. However, even if you use this protocol only with your unit, your colleague will benefit from hearing about your work and thinking about how to organize units in a values-consistent way.

Partner Protocol

1. Write a paragraph describing your next unit. In the paragraph, include *outcomes* (what your students will learn), *tasks* (what they'll do in order to learn), *resources* (what they'll use to help them learn), and *work products* (what they'll create to reinforce and demonstrate their learning).

2. Have your partner read your paragraph. Avoid making statements about why you've organized the unit as you have or explaining the unit in any other way. Your partner might wish to annotate your paragraph or take notes as you read it aloud.

3. Your partner describes the unit back to you without looking at the paragraph. Note any differences between what the paragraph says and what your colleague says, including omissions, additions, and rearranged sequences.

4. Your partner says back to you what seems important to you in this unit. This time, your partner can choose to look at the paragraph.

5. Optional: Switch roles and repeat the protocol from the beginning.

Reflection Questions

- How did it feel to write the paragraph? To share it? To hear your partner's description of your unit? To hear your partner's interpretation of your values?
- What mistakes did your partner make when retelling your unit? What might those mistakes tell you about the unit's tasks or sequence?
- What did your partner get right when retelling your unit? What might you learn from the fact that your partner understood and remembered these details?
- What might you add, take away, or change so that your unit better serves your values?

Variation

Instead of having your colleague read the entire paragraph, have them read just some of it and ask them to imagine the missing pieces. For example, Xiomara might show a colleague just the first part of a paragraph about her graphing functions unit, say that there will be a project, and then ask the colleague to imagine what the project could entail. If her colleague comes up with a project that serves functions similar to the one she's planning, then Xiomara knows that her project fits her unit. If her colleague imagines a completely different sort of project, she might need to redesign the project or more clearly explain how it fits into the unit.

Quarters

Teachers sometimes say they'd love to include a particular activity or assignment in their curriculum, but they don't have time. They might say things such as "If my class met five days a week instead of four, we'd do a lot more independent reading," or "They need at least thirty minutes of vigorous exercise a day, but by the time they've changed into their gym clothes, the period is half over," or "If we had a block schedule, we could do more labs," or conversely, "I don't know what I'd do with the kids for ninety minutes."

A school schedule—itself a reflection of someone's values—will encourage some types of learning tasks and discourage others. In "Maker's Schedule, Manager's Schedule," programmer and artist Paul Graham (2009) argues that traditional workplace schedules, broken into hour-long increments, allow managers to slot meetings into each hour, but makers need longer blocks of time to create their work, edit, get feedback, look at other people's work to get ideas, revise some more, or even start over—and that does not account for setup and clean-up time. In schools, we might expect to see a maker's schedule so that students have time for sustained exploration and creation, yet we often see a manager's schedule, especially for older students.

But just because certain scheduling decisions *encourage* some learning tasks over others doesn't *require* us to use those tasks or prevent us from exploring other possibilities. If you watch reality competition shows, you see chefs preparing gourmet meals in thirty minutes and fashion designers creating avant-garde dresses in less than a day. Although you see contestants' ambitious ideas fail because the clock runs out, you also witness near-miracles of creativity on these shows. Teachers, like reality-show contestants, usually aren't able to choose how much time we have, but we usually do have some say in how we use that time. Instead of choosing learning tasks based on how much time *they take*, we can make values-based decisions about how *we use* the time we have.

The following exercise, *Quarters*, helps you assess how well your unit's learning tasks serve your values and imagine more values-consistent ways to organize your unit. You'll need a copy of your unit plan, a pen, and a highlighter.

Individual Exercise
1. Read through your unit plan. Write down the number of days or minutes you've allotted to your current unit.
2. Divide that number of days or minutes by four.
3. Imagine that you had to decrease the days or minutes in your unit by one quarter. If you had that much less time, what would you cut from your unit? That is, if you had to teach this same unit in 75 percent of the time,

what would you cut or change? On your unit plan, highlight the things you would cut completely, shorten, or modify.

4. Now imagine that you had to increase the days or minutes in your unit by one quarter. If you had that much more time, what would you add to your unit? That is, if you had to teach the same unit in 125 percent of the time, what would you add or change? On your unit plan or on a separate page, write what you'd add, expand, or take to the next level.

Reflection Questions
- What would happen if you replaced the quarter of your unit you'd cut with the quarter you'd add?
- What's stopping you from replacing the quarter of your unit you'd cut with the quarter you'd add?
- Consider the parts you'd add. What values do they serve? How can you more fully enact these values in your teaching—regardless of whether you change this unit?

Extension

After planning your next unit, use *Quarters* as a reflective exercise again, and then use it again after the following unit. After you've done the exercise with several successive units, look for patterns in the kinds of learning experiences you wish you could add and cut. What's preventing you from making these changes? What book can you read, or what workshop can you attend, to get ideas for how to overcome these obstacles? Which of your colleagues can you talk to?

Grading Your Unit

Just as you might grade your students' work based on how well it matches a set of standards, you can grade your own work. In this case, the work you're grading is your unit plan and the standards you're using come from your own values.

For the exercise, you'll first identify values you think are most important for your students to enact. Then, you'll give your unit a grade based on how well you think it provides students with opportunities to enact those values. The grade will help you consider making adjustments to your unit so that it provides even more meaningful learning experiences for your students.

Figure 5.3 (below) has a unit-grading rubric for you to fill out during the exercise. You'll also need a copy of your unit plan.

Individual Exercise

1. From the list in appendix A (p. 187), choose three to five values that you believe are most important for your students to enact in your classroom. Write these in the first column of the Unit-Grading Rubric (figure 5.3, below) under *Values*.

2. Read through your unit plan and consider how, as it's currently organized, it provides opportunities for your students to enact each of these values.

3. Give your unit a series of grades that indicate how well it provides opportunities for your students to enact each value. Use the same grading scale you use for your students—whether that's a letter grade, a percentage score, a point value, or a verbal description. Write these in the second column of the Unit-Grading Rubric under *Grades*.

VALUES	GRADES
To me, a unit is meaningful when it provides opportunities for students to use, develop, or show the following qualities of action.	How well did the unit provide opportunities for students to enact this value?

FIGURE 5.3
Unit-Grading Rubric

Reflection Questions

- How did it feel to grade your unit with respect to each of your values?
- Were you surprised by any of the grades you gave yourself? Which ones? Why?
- Based on the grades you've given yourself, are there changes you want to make to your unit? For example, do you want to replace certain learning experiences with others? Do you want to change how you've allocated time?
- At any point, did you find yourself feeling defensive or wanting to justify why your unit got a lower grade than you would have liked? This defensiveness isn't bad and doesn't necessarily mean you need to change your unit. Rather, it suggests that another important value is at stake. Can you name that value? Can you think of ways to bring that value to other units?
- Did some values get lower grades than you would have liked, but you're not sure how to serve them better? Which colleague might you observe or talk to for ideas about how to serve this value in other units or future years?

Extension

After teaching your unit, you might have your students identify values that make learning meaningful for *them* and grade the unit based on those criteria. They might make interesting suggestions for how you can make the unit more meaningful. Perhaps more importantly, you can use this exercise as an opportunity to help them consider how they might bring their own values to their learning, regardless of how their teachers organize units.

ONWARD

In this chapter, we explored how to organize a unit so that it leads to meaningful learning. In the next chapter, we'll see how to assess that learning.

6

Use Values to Assess Learning

Nancy, a choral music teacher, would like to see whether her students understand musical notation. She has many options for how she can assess their understanding. She could give a written quiz where her students label notes on a staff. She could play a short piece and have the students transcribe it in musical notation. She could have each student write a description of musical notation. She could give the students pieces of sheet music and have them sight-sing, meaning they'd sing the correct notes when looking at the sheet music for the first time.

We sometimes use the word *assessment* as if it refers to a physical thing—as in "My students did poorly on their *assessment*," or "I'm giving an *assessment* this Friday." But assessment isn't a thing; it's a *function* of a thing. To assess students, we ask them to perform a task that makes their understandings and skills observable and measurable. That's why this chapter refers to assessment *tasks*. Students perform a task, and one function of that task is to provide the basis of assessment.

If you want to assess students—to see and measure what they know and can do—many different possible tasks will serve that function. At the same time, any *one* task can serve *many* functions. If Nancy asks her students to sight-sing a piece of music, she might be serving some or all of these functions: (1) seeing how well her students understand musical notation, (2) giving them practice doing a real-world task that actual musicians do, (3) enabling the students to hear each other, and (4) allowing herself to give grades on the spot so she won't have to bring home work.

Most of these functions relate to student learning. If we asked Nancy to identify some of her values, she might say that growth, relevance, and appreciation matter to her. By giving the sight-singing task, Nancy also is serving values related to personal well-being by limiting the amount of work she must take home.

Nancy's colleague in the music department, Hector, gives a written quiz where students label notes on a staff. Even though the form of assessment is different, one function is the same: he, too, is seeing how well his students understand musical notation. His task serves the following additional functions: (1) providing a tangible record of progress that the students can store and access easily, (2) enabling his students to self-assess with an answer key, and (3) allowing him to grade the quizzes at home when he can concentrate and be more accurate.

Again, most of these functions relate to student learning. If we asked Hector about his values, he might say he cares about growth (just like Nancy), as well as accessibility, autonomy, and fairness. You might have strong feelings about which of these two tasks is the better assessment tool, but neither is inherently *right*. A good assessment task successfully makes visible that your students have learned important concepts and skills. Put differently, an assessment task works if it effectively serves your values.

The term *nutrient density* refers to how much nutrition (protein, vitamins, minerals, and so on) is packed into a given food. Orange soda and orange juice have about the same number of calories per ounce, but the juice gives you vitamin C and potassium whereas the soda gives you nothing nutritionally useful. Given that your time with your students is limited, you can make each assessment task *values-dense*, serving as many values as possible.

In this chapter, we'll first explore how to choose a values-dense assessment task—that is, a task that will help you see and measure what you think is most important for your students to have learned during a unit. Next, we'll consider how you can define what *success* means on a task, so that after your students complete it, you'll be able to articulate how well they did, according to your values. Finally, we'll see how you can set up your students for success on the assessment task.

LEARNING TASKS AS ASSESSMENT TASKS

Assessing means observing and measuring what students know and can do. Therefore, any task that has students demonstrate their knowledge and skills can serve as the basis of assessment. Many teachers give tests and quizzes that require students to draw upon their knowledge and skills in order to respond correctly or satisfactorily to a series of questions or prompts. But a test or quiz is only one of many ways to see what your students know and can do.

During any unit, students will engage in receptive learning tasks (when they take in new information) and expressive learning tasks (when they do something with that information). For example, students in Nancy's music classes take in new information by hearing a melodic phrase, and then they do something with what they learned: they sing the phrase. In other classes, students might watch a coach's batting stance and then try it themselves, read a book and then discuss its themes, or collect data on a paper airplane's velocity and then write a report about their findings.

Any expressive learning task will result in some sort of output, whether it's a song, a stance, a discussion, a lab report, or any other product. The work *process* serves as an instructional task, in that students learn from doing it, but the work *product* can serve as the basis for assessment. When reading a composition, watching a performance, seeing a display, or otherwise interacting with student work product, the teacher can determine whether the student understood the content, mastered the skills, and made meaning. In other words, you don't have to create an assessment task in addition to the expressive learning tasks you assign throughout the unit; you can assess the products of that work.

That said, you might decide *not* to use products of expressive learning tasks for assessment, and instead assess students' knowledge and skill development in another way. If students know that you'll evaluate and grade their work products, they might take fewer creative risks in an effort to give the right answers and please you.

Also, a complex expressive learning task might call upon skills you *aren't* assessing but that will affect how successfully students perform skills you *are* assessing. Imagine, for example, that a French teacher sets up a café at the end of every unit, so her students can celebrate their accomplishments and practice the new skills they've learned. At the end of the clothing unit, the teacher asks her students to describe outfits they'd wear for their dream jobs, compliment each other's outfits, and explain how that day's outfit reflects their identities.

These conversation topics give students an opportunity to review clothing vocabulary as well as grammatical constructions they've learned in previous units. Having these conversations also calls upon skills unrelated to French-speaking, such as visualizing a career path, giving an appropriate compliment, and thinking metaphorically. The teacher should make sure her students learn these skills so they can have successful conversations, but these aren't skills the teacher will assess. At the same time, the students' strengths or weaknesses in these areas might affect their ability to talk about clothing in French. In this case, the teacher might decide to give a separate, simpler assessment task, such as a traditional quiz on clothing vocabulary.

Another situation that might call for a separate assessment is when students create work product in groups. In a group, individuals might contribute according to their strengths, thus creating a product that represents the best of each student's skills. For example, in a history class, students might work in groups to create illustrated timelines of the industrial age. A student with a lot of art experience might make the drawings, while a student who's good at researching might find the information, and a student with strong writing skills might decide how to phrase that information on the timeline.

Such collaborations create the potential for students to learn from one another, generate ideas together, appreciate each other's strengths, and make the best possible work product. However, a group-made work product will not necessarily reveal each individual's skills in every area. Group performances also can obscure individuals' strengths, such as in a chorus that sounds off-key even when some singers hit their notes perfectly, or in a presentation where one person fails to prepare and the others get flustered and make mistakes. If you want to assess individual students' capabilities, give a separate task that they complete independently.

ASSESSING WHAT MATTERS

When you create assessment tasks, take care to assess the skills and understandings you think are important, as opposed to what's easy to see and measure. Imagine that Mila, a seventh-grade math teacher, uses the essential question *How can I use unit rates to help me make decisions?* for her unit on ratios, rates, and proportions. After teaching her students how to calculate unit rates, she poses the following problem: "I am trying to decide among three different cars to buy. I live in Brooklyn and drive to the Bronx every weekday, and I take longer trips to visit my family during the summer. I have a limited budget for gas and for the car itself, and I want to keep my emissions low. Which car would be the most cost-effective option for me?"

She shows her students how to research car prices and miles-per-gallon rates, map her yearly highway and city mileage, and set up algebraic equations to calculate her approximate yearly gas expenditures in order to figure out which car she should buy. On their unit test, the students successfully use cross products to solve proportions, convert between fractions or decimals and percentages, and use equations to solve word problems. A few days after the unit ends, Mila's principal notices the essential question still posted on her wall. He asks a student, "So, how *can* you use unit rates to help you make decisions?" The student, who's getting an *A* in math, can't answer.

Mila values teaching her students how they can use algebra in real life, and her essential question—*How can I use unit rates to help me make decisions?*—reflects that value. But the test only tells her how well her students can solve algebra problems, not whether they understand the bigger idea of using unit rates to help them make decisions.

If your task assesses what's easy to measure instead of valued understandings, you won't know if your students got the bigger idea, and your students might think the easy-to-measure stuff was the point. If you can't tell from a particular task whether students got the bigger idea, either change the task so it makes valued understandings visible, or create a series of tasks that measure different understandings.

Next year, Mila might create a project for which the students use rates, proportions, and percentages to help them make decisions in their own lives. Choosing a car might be relevant for Mila herself, but it isn't a decision her thirteen-year-old students are making. Mila could demonstrate the math using the car problem and then give them another problem to work on independently or in groups. Or she could guide her students through brainstorming ways they could use unit rates to help them make decisions, such as which phone plan would be most cost-effective, or which snacks would fit their levels of activity. Students could report on how they used rates, proportions, and percentages to help them make their decisions and how they could use similar math to help them make other kinds of decisions as they get older. If, after all of that, Mila needs to assess her students' use of the algebra further, she can give the test, too.

The revised Bloom's taxonomy (Krathwohl, 2002) distinguishes six levels of thinking: recall, comprehension, application, analysis, evaluation, and synthesis. Assessing student learning gets harder for us the higher students go on Bloom's scale; we can see much more easily whether students *correctly* recalled information or grasped a concept than determine how *effectively* they applied understandings to new situations, analyzed how a thing's parts relate to each other and to the whole, made judgments based on criteria, or created original work. However, if we teach knowledge and skills so that our students can *use* them for a meaningful purpose, then it makes sense for our tasks to demand higher-level processes, even if the products are harder for us to assess.

DEFINING WHAT SUCCESS MEANS

Once you've selected an assessment task for your students, you need to define what *successful performance* means. Even for a relatively simple assessment task such as Nancy's sight-singing quiz, students need to understand what *success* means in order to be successful. Does rhythm matter, or only pitch? If a student sings the notes a little flat but recognizes them all, would they still be considered successful? What if they sing too quickly or slowly? The answers to such questions might be obvious to Nancy but not to her students.

If you articulate your expectations clearly, students will know what to strive for, and you'll be able to hold them accountable. Figures 6.1 (p. 109), 6.2 (p. 110), and 6.3 (p. 111) have examples of assignment guidelines that articulate expectations in different ways. The first two include performance scales for each criterion, one with a number of points and the other with verbal descriptions; the third simply describes success and failure. All three teachers have communicated what they'll be valuing when they assess the work.

In writing your own guidelines, you can set up your students for success by defining your expectations but leaving some decisions for your students, weighting expectations so your students know which aspects matter most, and copying important expectations from one assignment to the next.

Unit: **GRAPHING FUNCTIONS IN THE COORDINATE PLANE**

Assignment: **DISCOVERING THE RELATIONSHIP**

Working in a group, you'll determine if there is a functional relationship, a correlation, or no relationship between two variables of interest to middle schoolers. For example, you might explore the relationship between hours of sleep and grades, money spent on clothes and self-esteem, or time spent with friends and happiness. You'll collect data, make a graph, present it to your classmates, and put the graph and a description of your findings on a mini-poster, which you'll copy and post in strategic places around the school to raise awareness about the issue.

ELEMENTS	CRITERIA	POINTS
RESEARCH QUESTION	You explored a question of of interest to middle schoolers for which you can determine if there is a relationship between variables.	/2
DATA COLLECTION	You collected enough data to be able to see on a graph whether there is a functional relationship, a correlation, or no relationship between the variables.	/3
DATA DISPLAY	Your scatterplot graph, best-fit line, and equation in slope-intercept form clearly and accurately showed the relationship between your variables.	/5
PRESENTATION	You explained your graph to your classmates verbally and algebraically.	/5
	You used appropriate volume and spoke clearly during your presentation.	/1
MINI-POSTER	You used your classmates' comments and our class discussion to help you write a clear explanation of your findings and suggestions for behavior based on the data.	/3
	You put your graph and description into a clear and eye-catching mini-poster.	/1

FIGURE 6.1
Discovering the Relationship Rubric

Unit: **CONFLICT TAKES THE STAGE**

Assignment: **DRAMATIC SCENE**

Using *A Raisin in the Sun* (Hansberry, 1994/1959) as a model, write a scene, intended for performance on the stage, dramatizing a conflict that is based on a real-life, first-hand experience with injustice.

When I read your scene, I will look MOST OF ALL for these elements:	BASIC	EFFECTIVE	EXEMPLARY
You draw on personal experiences to make your characters **authentic** rather than stereotypes.			
The conflict involves characters dealing personally with a **social injustice**.			
Each character has a **distinct voice**, conveyed through vocabulary, sentence structure, rhetorical devices, or some combination.			
I will ALSO look for these elements:	BASIC	EFFECTIVE	EXEMPLARY
The **set description and any stage directions** show an awareness of the stage and audience.			
An **in media res beginning** gets the audience to care about the characters and conflict right away.			
The **ending** leaves the audience thinking about the larger theme (the social injustice).			
The scene uses **playwriting conventions**: character names are in all-caps, and stage directions are in parentheses and italics.			
The scene's **title** engages the audience's interest and relates to the scene's topic or theme.			
The scene is **easy to read** because there are no errors in capitalization, punctuation, or spelling.			

FIGURE 6.2
Dramatic Scene Rubric

Unit: **THE CHESAPEAKE BAY WATERSHED**

Assignment: **WATER QUALITY INDICATORS LAB REPORT**

You and your partner have collected and tested water from the Anacostia River. You will now write a lab report to share your findings.

You give a clear, specific explanation of the purpose of testing water quality.	You give a vague or unclear explanation of the purpose of testing water quality.
You explain your hypothesis for how clean our water is, based on your knowledge from this course.	You write a hypothesis that doesn't fit what you've learned and/or is unclear.
You thoroughly and accurately describe the materials and procedure you used.	You describe the materials and procedure incompletely or confusingly, so that a reader cannot understand what you did.
You organize observations and data in clear and accurate charts and tables.	You present observations and data in an unclear, disorganized, or inaccurate way.
In your discussion, you use data to support conclusions about the water quality.	You draw conclusions without referring to data to support them, or your conclusions are not supported by the data.

FIGURE 6.3
Water Quality Indicators Lab Report Rubric

Define Your Expectations but Leave Some Decisions for Your Students

Students need parameters that are open-ended enough that they can take ownership of their work, yet defined enough that they understand your expectations and aren't overwhelmed by infinite possibilities.

Imagine that in a physical science class, eighth graders use common household items to build bridges. The bridges must carry a load of at least fifteen kilograms but can weigh no more than a hundred grams and be no longer than thirty centimeters. After the students test their bridges' strength, the class makes a scatterplot graph of each bridge's efficiency ratio—the mass the bridge can hold relative to the mass of the bridge itself. On posters, the students display photos of real-world bridges of the same type as their models, written discussions of their design processes, and charts of their data.

The bridge project is defined enough that students understand what excellence means, yet it leaves room for creative use of materials and design, and for friendly competition over whose bridge will hold the most weight. More generally, you can define parameters that help students complete the project and successfully demonstrate the knowledge and skills you think are important but leave other content or process choices to them.

Weight Expectations Based on Your Values

For most assignments, you have several different expectations, but not all expectations will matter equally. You can make sure that your students know which aspects of their work you think are most important, both by telling them on the assignment guidelines and by devoting the most class time to teaching students the skills they need to be successful in those areas.

When Vita's students read *A Raisin in the Sun* (Hansberry, 1994/1959), they look closely at how the playwright creates authentic characters who have distinct voices and deal personally with societal conflicts. When writing their own dramatic scenes, Vita's students spend class time learning how to make each character's voice sound distinct and authentic rather than generic and stereotypical, and how a societal conflict might come up in someone's personal life. These are the very elements Vita looks for most when she assesses her students' scenes. She looks for other things, too, but what gets the most class time also gets the most weight in their grades.

Mila has a different system for giving values-congruent grades. She has her math students write explanations of where they went astray on problems they got wrong, and then they redo the problems correctly and get back at least some of their points. Mila values thoroughness and self-discipline in the problem-solving process, so she doesn't give partial credit. She values self-awareness, so her students analyze their own errors; and resourcefulness, so they figure out for themselves how to get the correct solution. Finally, she values high achievement, so she doesn't let her students off the hook with only partially correct work.

Copy Valued Expectations from Assignment to Assignment

Every time Jill's eighth graders write an essay, she teaches them how to use specific evidence to support their points. By the end of the year, her students can recite her expectation verbatim—"You support your thesis with specific evidence"—because it's been on every essay assignment rubric, and they know it's an important aspect of writing a strong essay.

Because each assignment is different, Jill tells her students what kind of evidence they should include in each essay. Her assignment sheet for essays about neighborhood success stories says, "You support your thesis with specific evidence. *In this case*, your evidence should include images and stories of someone or something successful in your neighborhood." Later in the year, when her students write essays about activists whose memoirs they read, the assignment sheet says, "You support your thesis with specific evidence. *In this case*, your evidence should include images and stories of your activist." Copying guidelines from one assignment to the next, but specifying how each assignment is different, helps students understand what it means to do well.

SETTING UP STUDENTS FOR SUCCESS ON ASSESSMENT TASKS

Assessment tasks often demand substantial effort, and the product at least potentially matters—within and beyond your class, now and in the future, to the student personally and in the world. Out of respect for the effort that goes in, and the significance that comes out, we can position all students to complete assessment tasks successfully by providing the following.

A description of the assignment

You should be able to describe an assessment task in a sentence or two. For his music quiz, Hector might describe the task as "Label each note's pitch and value." A more complex task likely will require a more complex description, such as the one in figure 6.2 (p. 110): "Using *A Raisin in the Sun* (Hansberry, 1994/1959) as a model, write a scene, intended for performance on the stage, dramatizing a conflict that is based on a real-life, firsthand experience with injustice."

A list of criteria for excellence

To complete a project successfully, students need to know what *success* means. In listing qualities of a well-done product, you might include formal specifications ("The poster includes *at least six images of plants and animals that live in your biome*") and functional specifications ("The poster *convinces the viewer to preserve this biome* by showing or describing how humans have impacted it").

A list of criteria serves not only as an assignment rubric for students but also as a unit plan for you. Whatever you expect students to understand or do in order to complete their work successfully, you'll teach explicitly during the unit. The more important the expectation, the more lessons you'll devote to strategy instruction, so that students know how to do a particular task, such as finding good images online or describing human impacts on a biome—or more generally, how to find or generate ideas, make or assemble the work, decide what to add or change, spot and fix mistakes, give and receive feedback, and know when they're finished.

Just because an assessment task looks like a real-world task, doesn't mean your criteria for excellence must be the same as in the real world. Consider a sixth-grade physical education class that competes in their own basketball tournament, timed to coincide with the National College Athletic Association's tournament. But rather than focus on which team wins or how many points each student gets—success criteria for college players—the sixth-grade teachers rate each student's competencies in dribbling, passing, shooting, and other basketball skills, as well as in fair play, leadership, and other relational skills.

On the day you begin a new unit, let your students know what the major assessment task will be. That way, as they work through the unit, they know what they will be asked to do to demonstrate their learning. By the time you give out the list of guidelines, your students already will have started working on the assignment.

Multiple exemplars so students can see what excellence looks like

Whether your students' task is to write papers on the Arab Spring or print properly formed lowercase letters, they need to see what the end products should look like. But students who see only one exemplar might not know which aspects are fundamental qualities of the product and which are idiosyncratic to that example.

Imagine a fifth-grade teacher who wants his students to write articles about personal encounters with wildlife. He has trouble finding nature articles written at a fifth-grade reading level that have the scientific and literary quality he wants his students to achieve, so he decides to write his own. It's about a time when he visited the Galapagos and watched two marine iguanas fight, and the conclusion has a line about how he wanted to help the iguanas make peace even though he knew it was silly to anthropomorphize animals.

Although he has his students brainstorm lots of ways they could conclude their articles, about a third of the students write that they anthropomorphized the animals they encountered. If the students had opportunities to analyze multiple exemplars, they would have discovered more ways nature writers conclude articles and would have been better equipped to use their creativity within the bounds of the assignment—and less likely to plagiarize their teacher's work.

All required materials

Assessment tasks sometimes require materials not normally available in the classroom and not on a traditional school supply list. If your students were going to make board games or three-dimensional models to show what they know about the content they learned in your class, would you have the necessary materials? If not, what would you do? Ask the parents to buy them? That privileges students whose parents have the time and money to shop. Get them yourself? That adds to your workload and budget. Enlist your colleagues to bring in stuff? Now you're putting them out.

Like many practical matters at school, planning assessment tasks goes best when you have the combined knowledge, skills, and resources of a group. Maybe your colleagues will have ideas for how you can get the materials you want easily and cheaply, or they'll have a different idea for materials you can use.

Sufficient in-class work time for students to reach the expected level of quality

To create meaningful products, students need time for individual or group work, peer and teacher conferencing and coaching, and ad-hoc mini-lessons. One way to help students make the most of a work period is to have them set goals for themselves. If they write their goals, you can check them quickly and then support students who need to make their goals more specific, achievable, or appropriate to the assignment. For example, if a student says she wants to use a science work period to "go over" her lab report, the teacher could ask what aspect she's looking to strengthen and what revision strategy she plans to use—and teach her one if necessary. As the period continues, you can monitor students' progress toward their goals and have them set new ones.

Another way to manage a class during a work period is to have each student sign up to do a particular type of work. For example, art students working on metalsmithing could sign up to review soldering with the teacher, partner up for peer critiques, or work individually on hammering their pieces. Posting sign-ups allows you to see at any moment whether your students are on or off task.

Opportunities, but not an obligation, to share

By definition, an assessment task results in work that you will see and evaluate. However, if students create work that has personal significance, they might want to share their work with a wider audience—perhaps with loved ones, classmates, students at other schools, community stakeholders, or practitioners in the field they studied. You can research ways to make your students' work more public using apps, websites, newsletters, displays, and events. The possibility of publication might motivate some students to improve their work.

At the same time, if the product matters to them, it might also invoke their vulnerabilities. Imagine that, given the assignment to write a one-act play about a personal connection to a societal injustice, a gay student chooses to write about keeping his sexual orientation secret from his biological father. He's comfortable sharing this experience with his teacher, but he might not want to share his play with his classmates. If you give your students choices about whether and how they share, you show them that their work is worth sharing and that it's *theirs* to share—or not.

TOOLS FOR USING VALUES TO ASSESS LEARNING

We've seen how to choose a values-dense assessment task, define for students what it means to complete that task successfully, and set up students to succeed. This chapter's tools will help you assess your assessment tasks, according to your values. In *Assessment Task Swapping*, you'll clarify how well an assessment task serves your values and decide whether you want to swap that task for another that serves your values even better. *Assessment Filter* helps you distinguish success standards that serve your values from those that serve your preferences. *Assessing Your Rubric* includes a rubric you can use to assess rubrics you give your students.

Assessment Task Swapping

Assessment, or finding out what students understand and can do, can always be accomplished through many different tasks. This exercise is an opportunity for you to more fully understand an assessment task's many functions, evaluate the extent to which the task serves your values, and imagine new possible tasks that might better serve your values. The point isn't necessarily to *change* your assessment practices but rather to *notice* how values-dense different tasks are. If nothing else, you'll clarify for yourself why your current task is a values-dense one.

During the exercise, you'll list the task's functions—the things it *does*. Many tasks have instructional *and* assessment functions: students learn concepts and skills in performing the task, and the end product is what the teacher looks at to see how much the student learned. The process of painting a portrait, playing a soccer game, doing a lab experiment, having a conversation in Chinese, or taking a multiple-choice history test helps students learn the skills to do these tasks so they'll be better at them the next time they do something similar.

Even if you give a task purely for assessment purposes, students will learn content and skills while performing it. For example, if students write an essay *after* learning about the Vietnam War, they'll learn more about the war *while* writing the essay. As they take an algebra test, they're *learning* algebra as opposed to just demonstrating what they've learned already. That's because retrieving information "is not merely a readout of the knowledge stored in one's mind; the act of reconstructing knowledge itself enhances learning" (Karpicke & Blunt, 2011, p. 774). An instructional task helps students learn, and an assessment task shows the extent to which they learned, but students are *always* learning, even as they're being assessed.

Most tasks will have more instructional than assessment functions, because you probably won't assess everything students do. For example, an assignment to write an essay on the Vietnam War might have two assessment functions: the teacher sees (1) what students know about the war's causes and (2) how well they can organize their ideas. The task has instructional functions in these same two areas; by writing the essays, students will more fully understand the war's causes and get better at organizing their ideas. If students read each other's essays and offer feedback, then the task has an additional instructional function, which is to teach students how to give and use feedback. During this exercise, expect your list of instructional functions to include all of the items that appear on your list of assessment functions, plus more.

Individual Exercise

1. In a sentence or two, but no more than that, describe the task you currently use to assess student learning during your unit.
2. Identify all of the *assessment* functions of this task. That is, what skills and understandings does it reveal? Consider making separate lists in the following categories and any other categories that might be important to you:
   - Discipline-specific knowledge
   - Discipline-specific skills
   - Thinking skills
   - Communication skills
   - Relational skills
   - Organizational skills
3. Identify all of the *instructional* functions of the task. That is, what understandings will students develop, or what skills will they practice, while doing this task? Consider making lists in the same categories as in step 2, and note that most likely this list and the previous one will overlap.
4. Identify all of the *management* functions of the task. That is, how will giving this task help you use your time, energy, resources, and expertise most effectively?
5. Of all of the functions you identified in steps 2–4, circle the three that matter most to you.

6. Now, come up with a *different* assignment that would serve the three functions you've just circled. You might wish to consult the list of meaningful tasks in appendix B (p. 190) to get ideas, but use it to help you, not to limit you.
7. Make a list of all of the *other* assessment, instructional, and management functions this alternative assignment would serve.

Reflection Questions

- How would each task be a worthwhile use of your students' time?
- What important learning would each task reveal?
- If your students were able to complete each task successfully, what would they be able to do next?
- Which of your values would each task serve? You might refer to the list of values in appendix A (p. 187).
- Does it make sense to swap the task you currently use for one you don't?
- If it doesn't make sense to include this new task in your current unit, where else in your course might it go?

Extension

Russ Harris (2009) identifies some of the barriers to acting in accordance with our values: getting stuck in self-limiting beliefs, minimizing or disregarding what matters most, avoiding discomfort, and external circumstances. If you think the new task is more values-dense than the one you currently use but still feel hesitant, try going through potential barriers to using it: beliefs about yourself that might stop you from giving this assessment task, important learning outcomes or processes that you might be minimizing or disregarding, uncomfortable situations or feelings that this task might bring, and any external factors that might limit the task's feasibility. How significant are these barriers? Will they stop you? If you want to overcome them, who can help?

Assessment Filter

How students treat their time, their classroom, the work itself, each other, and themselves probably matters a great deal to you and might reflect some of your most deeply held values as an educator—but bad work habits don't necessarily mean bad work product. Similarly, requiring students to deliver their work by a certain time and in a certain format might help them learn organizational skills and might help keep *you* organized, but these considerations aren't the same as criteria for excellent work product. And although we all have preferences, students shouldn't have to make their work look or sound a certain way just because we like it.

When we assess student work, *some* expectations might reflect our values for excellent work product. Others might reflect our values for student behavior during the work process, our expectations for how they submit the work, or even our aesthetic preferences. This exercise is designed to help you filter your assignment expectations so that what you're left with are values-consistent criteria for excellent work.

Individual Exercise

1. Choose an assessment task you currently give. If you have a list of steps for performing the task or a rubric for evaluating its outcome, you may wish to take these out for reference.
2. For the first filter, consider how your *aesthetic preferences* might impact your assessment of the work product.
   - What do you expect the work to look like?
   - What materials do you expect students to use?
   - Do you require a certain layout or format? (For example, do you ask students to use certain fonts, spacing, binding, or headers?)
3. For the second filter, consider how your *submission expectations* might impact your assessment of the work product.
   - What format do you expect? A hard copy? A digital file? A certain file type?
   - Is there a specific deadline? What happens if a student turns in the assignment after that deadline? Are some students allowed to miss the deadline? Which excuses do you consider valid?
   - What delivery method do you ask students to use? For example, do you ask them to e-mail you their work? Share a document with you? Give you a physical copy?
4. For the third filter, consider how your *behavioral values* during the work process might impact your assessment of the work product.
   - Are students penalized for off-task behavior? Disruptive behavior? Absence from class?
   - Does attention-seeking or help-seeking behavior positively or negatively impact your evaluation of their work?

- Do you expect students to work in a particular place?
- Do you expect students to spend a particular amount of time working?
5. Now that you've filtered out your aesthetic, submission, and behavioral preferences, list criteria for excellent work.

Reflection Questions
- Which questions were hardest to answer? Why do you think that is?
- How do your criteria for excellent work match your values? You may wish to consult the list of values in appendix A (p. 187).
- Which design aesthetics do you think are integral to the work product? Which ones seem like personal preferences?
- Do some design choices reflect values, not preferences? Which values? If these design considerations are important, do you devote class time to teaching them? If not, why not?
- How can you make sure your students submit their work such that they respect your time and learn to respect other people's time—without conflating these expectations with your expectations for the work itself?
- How might you assess student behavior separately from academic skills and understandings?
- How will you communicate your values and preferences to your students?

Variation

Another way to separate out aesthetic preferences, submission expectations, and behavioral values is through drawing. Draw a cartoon that includes three panels: the ideal work product, a student turning in work in an ideal way, and a group of students displaying ideal behavior during the work process. What do you notice about your drawings? Would it be possible to turn in excellent work that doesn't look like the first image, isn't delivered in the manner displayed in the second image, and isn't the result of the behaviors depicted in the third image? Do the images reflect your values, goals, preferences, or some combination? How can you teach your students behaviors that matter? How can you assess those behaviors?

Assessing Your Rubric

A rubric is a communication tool. It tells students the qualities you look for when you examine and evaluate their work. That said, a rubric is only one of many tools you can use to help students succeed. Others include to-do checklists, pacing calendars, exemplars, revision strategy mini-lessons, coaching sessions, and peer feedback. But because rubrics describe criteria for successful work, they have the potential to be places where you clearly and definitively articulate your values to your students. This exercise is designed to help you do that, using the Rubric for Rubrics (figure 6.4, below).

Assignment: **WRITING A RUBRIC** Using rubrics you've encountered in and beyond this book as models, write a rubric to help your students understand criteria for excellence on an upcoming assessment task.			
Elements	BASIC	EFFECTIVE	EXEMPLARY
The rubric includes the **titles** of the unit and assignment so students see the assessment task as part of a larger learning experience.			
A brief (1–2 sentences) **assignment description** helps students clearly visualize their task.			
The rubric includes 3–7 important **criteria for excellence** so students understand where to devote their attention.			
The rubric **explains why each criterion matters** so students understand why to devote their attention to it.			
Various **design elements** such as fonts, tables, and graphics help students understand the rubric's information and do not distract or overwhelm the student.			
The rubric's language, organizational structure, and design elements are **consistent with other rubrics** used in the same course, so that students come to understand criteria for excellence in the discipline.			
The rubric **describes a product**, not a process. While there can and should be process instruction during class, details about the task's process (such as a step-by-step procedure, to-do list, or set of revision strategies) do not appear on the rubric itself.			

FIGURE 6.4
Rubric for Rubrics

Individual Exercise

1. Write a rubric for an upcoming assignment.
2. Evaluate the rubric's elements, using the Rubric for Rubrics (figure 6.4, p. 122).

Reflection Questions

- Based on your evaluation, how (if at all) will you revise your rubric? What might you cut, add, rearrange, or otherwise alter so that the rubric better reflects your values?
- Did you disagree with any of the criteria for what makes an excellent rubric? What values do those disagreements reflect?

Extension

The Rubric for Rubrics in figure 6.4 (p. 122) is a *single-point rubric* (Fluckiger, 2010); that is, it only describes one point in learning: proficiency. You also might be familiar with *analytic rubrics* (Nitko & Brookhart, 2007), which describe multiple levels of performance. The Discovering the Relationship Rubric in figure 6.1 (p. 109) and the Dramatic Scene Rubric in figure 6.2 (p. 110) are both single-point rubrics, because they only describe proficiency. The Water Quality Indicators Lab Report Rubric in figure 6.3 (p. 111) is an analytic rubric, because it describes both satisfactory and unsatisfactory performance. Some analytic rubrics include even more levels, and perhaps you've seen—or made—charts that describe excellent, good, fair, and poor performance for each of several criteria.

Education professor Thomas Guskey (2015) argues that the more performance levels we include, the less accurately we'll evaluate performance, because it's too easy to mistakenly assign one label as opposed to another. Percentage grades have a hundred levels of performance, which means we have ninety-nine opportunities to classify student performance inaccurately (Guskey, 2015). Letter grades seem to have only five levels of performance (A, B, C, D, and F), but the added pluses and minuses expand the number of levels to nine (A, A−, B+, B, B−, C+, C, C−, D, and F), which only leaves room for more judgment calls and therefore more mistakes (Guskey, 2015). That's why the Water Quality Indicators Lab Report Rubric in figure 6.3 (p. 111) describes only two levels of performance: satisfactory and unsatisfactory.

Allocating numbers of points to different criteria shows students how important the criteria are, relative to each other. The Discovering the Relationship Rubric in figure 6.1 (p. 109) uses numbers of points to show students that displaying and explaining their data are the skills that matter most. But if you use numbers of points this way, you open yourself up to making more judgment calls, and therefore more mistakes, in the very areas where you care most. Instead of assigning points, you can simply tell students what matters most, which is what the Dramatic Scene Rubric in figure 6.2 (p. 110) does.

As you continue to design rubrics, experiment with different ways to communicate which criteria matter most and what excellent performance entails, so that you'll equip your students to succeed.

ONWARD

In this chapter, we discovered how to create values-dense assessments that make visible the important ideas and skills students have learned. Now that we have spent several chapters exploring how your values can help you design meaningful units of study, we'll turn in the next chapter to how your values can help you develop your entire course.

7

Use Values to Design Courses

Debbie's tenth-grade visual arts course never looks the same way twice. Depending on her students' interests, she might have them use pencil, pastel, or charcoal. If a group works especially well together, she might have them assemble still lifes into one composition. If the spring weather is nice, she might send her students outside to paint *en plein air*. If a model is available, she might teach life drawing. Although she always teaches certain skills, such as how to do a color study or use negative space, the extent to which Debbie emphasizes them depends on the project and on each student's needs.

Regardless of what happens in any particular class, what Debbie most wants is for her students to relearn to see the world, so that instead of using symbols and stereotypes in their art, they represent actual shapes, colors, and textures. Debbie articulates these values as essential questions: *How do we see the world through observation rather than through labeling?* and *How do we represent what we see on two-dimensional surfaces?* These questions reflect Debbie's values as an art teacher and clarify her course's purpose, which she can then communicate to her students.

Another constant in Debbie's classes is her use of certain learning routines. No matter what projects her students do, she always begins with an exploration of the materials they will use, whether it's pencils or oil crayons or watercolors. Next, she has her students look at exemplars in photos, watch videos of artists, and—when possible—visit galleries or interview working artists in their studios. Every class period starts with students carefully arranging their workspaces, and every class ends with them cleaning up. On the first class of each month, Debbie shares local art happenings so that her students can learn from community members and see a future for themselves in the arts. Students come to expect these learning rituals, which help make the course a *course*, not just a set of projects.

Environmental scientist Donella Meadows (2008) defines a *system* as "an interconnected set of elements that is coherently organized in a way that achieves something" (p. 11). An academic course works as a system: it features an interconnected set of elements (units) that is organized coherently in a way that achieves something (meaningful learning).

Even if each unit has the integrity of a system, an overall course still can feel like a heap. One way to tell if your course is a heap is to give it a name. Can you call it something like *American History* or *Life Science*, which already sounds pretty broad in scope, or do you have to go even broader and call it something like *English 9*? Other than the fact that it's for ninth graders and that it's English (whatever *that* means), the course might not be organized coherently in a way that achieves something. It isn't a system; it's a heap.

Many courses are heaps of related topics, such as *American History* or *Life Science*. Education standards such as the Common Core, in contrast, relate mostly to skills so that students finish school with college, career, and civic readiness. Although education standards' emphasis on skills helpfully reminds us that students should learn how to *do* things rather than just absorb information, adding a skills scope and sequence on top of an existing topics scope and sequence doesn't do much to organize the curriculum into a system. If anything, the curriculum becomes more of a heap: now we have to cover the topics in the textbook *and* the skills in the standards.

Schools often face pressure to add more to the heap: more writing, more reading, more technology; more play time, but also more work time. More music and art and engineering and mindfulness and physical exercise and conflict-resolution training and test prep. How to make time for it all? More hours in the school day? More days in the academic year? More homework? (No, thanks.) And how do we make sure we're achieving *more*? More tests! No wonder teachers and students are exhausted by June.

With all that schools try to incorporate, courses easily can become heaps of topics, processes, and assignments. But if your students are to feel an ongoing sense of purpose and to learn in a way that is more likely to transfer to the next unit (or the next year), your entire course must be an interconnected, purposeful whole. A system.

In this chapter, we'll discover three ways to use your values to organize your course so it works as a meaningful system. First, ongoing strands tie the course together, making it feel like a continuous whole rather than a collection of units. Second, intentional variety in topics, processes, and assignments creates a sense of balance, so that the course serves multiple values over time. Third, the sequence of units can create a sense of meaningful progression, so that each unit builds on the last, and the course feels like a story with a beginning, middle, and end.

DESIGNING STRANDS TO CREATE A SENSE OF WHOLENESS

A course is more than the sum of its units. Consider a science teacher who incorporates the theme of diversity into every unit, a French teacher who gives weekly conversational skills checks, or an English teacher who has her students examine how each author they study constructs sentences that they then emulate in their own writing. We might call such elements *strands*; if units are the weft that gives a course its colors and patterns, strands are the warp that gives the course its structure and shape. Ongoing learning strands create continuity and a sense of wholeness in your course and are another way to teach by your values.

Just as units can be rehearsal-, project-, or inquiry-based, so can strands. Perhaps you incorporate certain practices into each unit, such as using grammar in context, checking work for errors, staying safe in a lab, or stretching before game play. You might even use certain practices during every lesson, or during certain kinds of lessons. For example, a math teacher might begin every class with a full-body stretch and then a challenge problem. When students are preparing for a test, she might end class by having students write lingering questions on slips of paper and then thank the classmates to their right and left for supporting them as they studied. Such routines orient students within the lesson or unit, and they set expectations for how students will treat their learning, their work, each other, and themselves.

Or perhaps your students work on a particular project all year, adding to it with every unit. Think of a wellness class that has units on cardio training, weightlifting, yoga, nutrition, and mindfulness. As an ongoing project, students design weekly wellness calendars for themselves, adding new practices as they learn about them in each unit, so that by the end of the course they've all created comprehensive and personalized programs they can use even after the course ends.

Strands can also be ongoing inquiries. In each unit, students might expand or qualify their thinking about a concept such as sustainability, discrimination, compassion, or evolution. Just as you can write essential questions for units, you can write them for your entire course. Course-level essential questions direct attention to what's most important in the discipline, elicit higher-order thinking about overarching themes, and pique students' curiosity about the subject. Examples of course-level essential questions include the following:

- English: *What defines an author's style?*
- Math: *When is "close enough" good enough?*
- Chemistry: *How can I make a reasonable prediction?*
- French: *How can I use grammatical and cultural conventions to communicate appropriately?*
- History: *How is now like then?*
- Music: *How do musicians respond to their environment when they play?*
- Art: *How do materials influence the artist's choices?*
- Physical Education: *What are an individual player's responsibilities on a team?*

Such questions might encompass entire academic programs. A question such as *What defines an author's style?* applies just as much when kindergarteners read Eric Carle's picture books as when seniors read a Toni Morrison novel. If you want to write essential questions for your course, try using the *Finding What's Essential* protocol in chapter 4 (p. 72–73), but discuss a course theme rather than a unit topic.

Overarching essential questions, ongoing projects, and recurring practices weave units together, especially when all of the units in a course are of a particular type. For example, like many art courses, Debbie's consists only of project-based units. But her materials exploration, exemplar analysis, and local art happenings strands introduce inquiry into her course, as do her overarching essential questions—*How do we see the world through observation rather than through labeling?* and *How do we represent what we see on two-dimensional surfaces?* When her students deliberately arrange and break down their work spaces, these actions serve as a rehearsal for becoming an artist (or any thoughtful practitioner). If your units are mostly inquiries, or mostly rehearsals, or mostly projects, strands can provide other kinds of meaningful learning experiences while also tying the units together.

DIVERSIFYING EXPERIENCES TO CREATE A SENSE OF BALANCE

Just as eating different healthy foods at different meals helps you fulfill your body's multiple needs, creating different learning experiences for different units helps you serve multiple values. If designing a single values-dense learning task is like choosing nutrient-dense orange juice over orange soda, designing a values-consistent task *mix* is like choosing a nutritionally balanced diet.

Just as your body needs more from certain food groups than others, your course might need more of certain task types than others. A Chinese teacher might give weekly spoken quizzes because he values oral fluency and wants his students to assess their own and each other's pronunciation and vocabulary. If he also values serving the community, he might have his students translate school documents or local information guides for Chinese-speaking families. This service-learning project might happen only once a year but still be enough to serve his and his community's values.

Beyond diversifying the tasks themselves, you can diversify the knowledge sources, materials, groupings, and stakes with which students perform the tasks.

Knowledge Sources

Educator Emily Style (1988) introduced the metaphor of "windows and mirrors" to describe how some curricular resources will reflect a given student's experiences whereas others will show less-familiar stories, ideas, and perspectives. Education professor Rudine Sims Bishop (1990) added to the concept by arguing that "window" texts can become "sliding glass doors, and readers have only to walk through in imagination to become part of whatever world has been created or re-created by the author" (p. ix).

Bishop (1990) explains the danger of not providing enough mirrors: "When children cannot find themselves reflected in the books they read, or when the images they see are distorted, negative, or laughable, they learn a powerful lesson about how they are devalued in the society of which they are a part" (p. ix).

Conversely, providing too *many* mirrors misleads students who share these identifiers into believing that their own experiences of the world are *right* or *normal*, and that anyone who doesn't share these identifiers is *lesser* or *other*. Providing a balance of resources shows students that no one way of thinking, looking, or being is *the* way.

What about your resources? How do the textbooks, images, videos, websites, maps, problem sets, case studies, guest speakers, and field trips your students encounter serve as mirrors of their own experiences and windows into less-familiar ones? How do they serve as sliding glass doors that your students can walk through, so that they don't just see unfamiliar experiences but empathize with the people who have lived them? How does your course provide an intentional variety of knowledge sources?

When considering the diversity among curricular resources, take care to avoid *tokenism*, or including resources by or about people with a minoritized status just to say you did; *illusory representation*, or promoting the belief that one person speaks on behalf of a group that person belongs to; *appropriation*, or using another culture's practice out of context and without respect for its significance; and *appeasement*, or including resources by or about people with a privileged status because those who share that status are used to having their perspective represented.

Materials

Some tasks inherently require particular materials. For example, making an oil painting requires paints, canvas, a palette, and brushes. Other tasks, such as a dance performance or spoken quiz, can be accomplished without any supplies. Students increasingly use electronic technology and digital tools to make slides and timelines, record audio and video, find images and opinions, write essays, play games, and take tests.

Choosing materials will create and remove valued possibilities. For example, engineering students using software to design a house of the future can revise their plans easily and share them widely, but using cardboard would provide physical feedback and a tangible product. Over time, their teacher might design a task mix that allows students to do some projects using software and others using cardboard. In your course, you can make values-based decisions about which materials students use for which assignments.

Group Sizes

Most tasks can be adapted for individual students, pairs, or groups. The group's size will create problems and possibilities. A larger group allows for more perspectives and ideas, but it also makes room for some students to take over, slack off, or have their ideas drowned out by more assertive peers. If your students work in groups, guide them to choose the values they want to bring to their group work. You also can create a balance of individual, partner, small group, and large group tasks so that students have all of these experiences—and the accompanying benefits and drawbacks.

Stakes

If you want your students to synthesize their understandings, then you might give one big assessment task. Although some students might feel stressed out by the prospect of performing one task that demonstrates all of the knowledge they've amassed over weeks or months, the process of distilling key understandings and then using them in a novel situation can be tremendously rewarding, and even exciting. Some students won't realize how much they've learned until they put the pieces together into a coherent whole.

Another option is to give smaller, lower-stakes tasks throughout a unit. If you give a lot of little quizzes and projects, these can reveal a student's capabilities at a given moment and show progress over time. In creating a mix of tasks, consider how you might balance smaller, more frequent tasks with larger, more cumulative ones.

You might think of other balances you want to create among your course's assignments—based on your subject matter, student population, and values.

SEQUENCING UNITS TO CREATE A SENSE OF PROGRESSION

Ayanna teaches sixth-grade American history and eighth-grade world geography. If she's asked about the scope and sequence of her courses, she says sixth grade goes from enslavement to the civil rights movement. Then she takes a deep breath and explains that in eighth grade, she goes by region, with units on Latin America, Africa, Europe, and Asia. At the end of the year, each student chooses a country to study in greater depth and does a project, culminating in World Day every June.

In her American history course, Ayanna teaches the content in chronological order. But the world geography course—like most courses—doesn't have an inherent order. Nothing about Latin America makes the fall an ideal time for studying it. The students don't need a foundational understanding of Latin American physical geography in order to learn about Africa; Latin

America just happens to come first in the textbook. Country studies could just as logically start the course as end it.

Course sequences are not fixed or intrinsic to the subject matter. Even history courses have no natural order; just because history happened in an order doesn't mean it must be taught in that order. Science teachers don't teach their content in the order in which it was discovered, and music isn't usually taught according to when it was composed. Course sequences are constructs, rooted in the values of those who make them up.

A course's sequence often is a matter of tradition. A unit might be associated with a particular time of year, such as a fall unit on farms that coincides with the harvest, a winter music unit that features holiday songs, or a spring physical education unit on baseball. Some course traditions seem arbitrary: "Fifth graders always have done mythology at the end of the year." And many courses follow a textbook.

Using a preexisting or traditional sequence isn't necessarily bad; it just is not the only possibility for your course, and a different sequence of units might move your students in a valued direction more effectively. When you put your units in an order, consider how you can create a meaningful progression.

Skills Progressions

Many teachers sequence their courses such that the early units establish foundational skills that later units build on, like how math teachers build on students' knowledge of geometry when they introduce trigonometric functions, or how first-grade teachers build on their students' ability to read fiction when they introduce informational texts. When you sequence your units, you might cluster those that demand similar skills so students have a chance to practice those skills intensively, or you might spread out those units so students regularly return to the skills and don't forget them.

Conceptual Progressions

In a single unit, essential questions direct your and your students' attention to important ideas. Over several units, or even your entire course, a series of essential questions can show students how these ideas build on each other. Consider how the following four essential questions, each of which shapes a separate unit in an English class, work together to create a deepening inquiry that spans the four units:

1. *How do our environments influence our definitions of success and our op-portunities to become successful?* Unit text: *Of Mice and Men* (Steinbeck, 1993/1937)
2. *How can people redefine success for themselves?* Unit texts: *The House on Mango Street* (Cisneros, 1991) and *Persepolis* (Satrapi, 2003)
3. *How does activism help ensure that everyone has a chance to be successful?* Unit text: choice of activist memoirs
4. *How can I use my writing as a form of activism?* Unit text: *A Raisin in the Sun* (Hansberry, 1994/1959)

Notice that the words *success* and *activism* deliberately echo through the essential questions to help students see how each unit builds on the last. When this English teacher first started teaching her course, the units were in a different order. She taught *The House on Mango Street* (Cisneros, 1991) relatively early in the year because it seemed like an easier book. Then, she taught *Of Mice and Men* (Steinbeck, 1993/1937) and *A Raisin in the Sun* (Hansberry, 1994/1959) back-to-back, not only because students find these texts more challenging but also because both books explore individual dilemmas brought about by systemic oppression. The activist memoir unit was her own addition to the curriculum, which she tacked on at the end of the year. But as she thought about these units' themes, she changed the order to create a more meaningful progression from how success is defined for people to how people define success for themselves to how they work to make success more accessible to everyone. She adjusted the wording of her essential questions to make this progression clear to her students and to herself.

Creating this sort of conceptual progression might mean rewording your essential questions to draw attention to important ideas that reappear throughout your course. You also might need to reorder your units so that students keep thinking about important ideas in different and deeper ways.

Even if your units are not inquiry-based and you therefore don't use essential questions, you still can sequence the units to create an ongoing inquiry. Imagine that after watching her colleague in the English department create a sustained inquiry about success and activism, Debbie wants to try something similar for her visual arts course. She'll still use project-based units, and she wants to stay flexible about the types of projects she gives, but she realizes that when the course consists of one seemingly random project after another, her students might feel like they've completed four projects and not like they've built a deeper understanding of artmaking. She comes up with a series of unit titles that articulate a thematic progression.

- Using Art to Tell My Story
- Using Art to Connect to My Community
- Using Art to Expand My Perspective
- Using Art to Effect Positive Change

The repeating element in these four titles (*using art to*) helps students see that each project, while different in topic and medium from the last, will teach them a new way that they can use art to do something meaningful. Art might be fun, but it isn't *only* for fun; it can also serve a purpose—and not just one purpose, but a variety of purposes. The four titles aren't in a random order; they move from *I* to *we*, and from reflecting the world to producing a better one. These units still leave room for Debbie to take advantage of available resources, current events, and students' interests. For example, students could approach almost any art project—whether it's a still-life drawing, a group mural, or a plein air painting—as an opportunity to connect to their communities. Creating this sequence for her course doesn't take anything away from it; it only adds a layer of meaning.

Work-Product Progressions

A third way to give your course a sense of progression is to have students create a series of similar yet increasingly sophisticated work products. Think of a science teacher who has his students keep observation journals for every phenomenon they study. For the first unit, on weather, they just write their observations each day. For the second unit, on animal life cycles, they write *and* draw their observations of tadpoles. For the third unit, on plant life cycles, they write and draw their observations of bean plants, and they also take and record measurements. By keeping the essential task the same and adding a component each time, the teacher helps his students see their scientist skills developing and gives his course a sense of forward motion.

Similar assignments don't have to recur in every unit, or even in consecutive units, to lend a sense of progression to your course. You can give similar tasks periodically, or bookend your course with two similar tasks. Consider a math teacher who begins his course by asking his students to conduct math interviews of adults they know. Students ask questions about how the adults use math in doing their jobs, caring for themselves and their families, maintaining their homes and belongings, and planning for their futures. The students then write essays about how their interviewees use math. At the end of the year, they do a similar project on how adults use math in their daily lives, but this time they imagine themselves as the adults using math, and instead of writing essays, they make comics with different panels representing different ways their future selves will use some of the math they've learned in and beyond the course. Giving meaningfully similar yet different assignments helps students see how much they've learned while reinforcing each assignment's purpose.

A third way to create progression through successive assignments is to use upcycling. Upcycling involves using something old and worn out (like a tweed jacket from the '70s) as raw material to make something new and better (like a cute purse). The term was coined by designers William McDonough and Michael Braungart, whose books *Cradle to Cradle* (2002) and *The Upcycle* (2013) describe how to design things so they not only last but can also eventually be put to new and better uses.

Though all teachers make use of prior *knowledge*—as when a math teacher builds on students' understanding of integers in a subsequent unit on equations—teachers rarely make use of past *work products*. More often, students take their work home to be displayed, filed, or thrown out.

Instead, the products of student learning from one unit can be upcycled in a future unit. Inspired by her own eighth-grade geography course, Ayanna decides to begin her sixth-grade history course with a unit on North American physical geography, so that students will be able to visualize the places where historical events occurred. At the end of the geography unit, her students make dioramas to illustrate different regions. Then, during a later unit on expansionism, she has her students use a green screen to make videos of themselves inside their own dioramas, pointing out features as they describe how American settlers interacted with the land and its inhabitants.

Upcycling has potential benefits beyond bringing a sense of progression to your course. If students see that the things they create for school can be upcycled, they might find that their work products, and the processes of making them, feel more worthwhile. Upcycling also gives students an authentic reason to reassess their creations, refine their thinking, and bring new and better ideas into their work. What do your students make? How could they upcycle these work products as meaningful parts of later units? How could you take advantage of your unit sequence—or how could you resequence your units—so your students can upcycle their work from one unit to the next?

UNDERSTANDING YOUR COURSE IN THE CONTEXT OF A LARGER PROGRAM

In nature, you find systems within systems, such as cells making up organs making up organisms making up ecosystems. You also see systems within systems in the human-made world: a household within a neighborhood within a city, or a shoe department within a clothing store within a chain. A curriculum, too, is made up of systems within systems. Units make up courses, which make up academic programs.

Even if your course by itself feels totally coherent, perfectly balanced, and meaningfully sequenced, the overall program it belongs to might lead you to rethink it. Imagine that Debbie is given wrapping paper from a party supply store and decides to do a collage project. One day during this project, a student says, "I feel like I never really understood what collages even were before I took this class. I thought it was just gluing a bunch of pictures to a piece of paper. But now I get how it's about making all the materials work together and really say something." Debbie realizes that her students usually work in a single medium, whether it's marker or acrylic paint or charcoal pencil, but they hardly ever do mixed-media projects—not just in her class but in any of their art classes. She decides that her course will always include a mixed-media project, not so much to create balance within the course itself, but to address a gap in the overall program.

As a teacher, you might not have the decision-making power to change entire programs, but you can get curious about how your program works. That way, you equip yourself to make values-based decisions about how your course operates inside that program. As you get curious about your program, look for gaps that your course could fill and meaningful arcs that your course could help to build.

Filling Programmatic Gaps

Can you think of topics, concepts, perspectives, or practices that matter to you but seem underrepresented in the curriculum—or that are missing entirely?

Maybe you think your students don't move their bodies enough, or engage in enough imaginative play, or build enough things with their hands. Maybe you think your students don't learn enough about recent historical events, or study enough grammar, or learn enough about art or science. Maybe you feel that your program focuses too much on academic skills and not enough on social skills. And maybe you think none of these things, because *not enough* according to one person's values might be *enough* or even *too much* according to another's.

One way to find gaps in your subject-area or grade-level curriculum is to make a values map: a document showing the parts of an academic program that serve a particular value. Although the idea of mapping your academic program might seem daunting, it doesn't have to include a lot of detail to be helpful. Any map should include only the information it needs to serve its purpose. If you want to show your mother-in-law how to get from your house to the local convenience store, a rough map drawn in fifteen seconds would serve its purpose just as well as if you took an hour to add detail. A values map, too, should be only as detailed as necessary to serve its purpose, which is to reveal gaps in the curriculum.

Figures 7.1 (p. 138) and 7.2 (p. 139) show two different examples of values maps. The map in figure 7.1 (p. 138) shows collaboration in an eighth-grade program; the map in figure 7.2 (p 139) shows sustainability in a science program. Neither map is especially long or detailed, but both illuminate values that matter to the teachers who made them.

To make your own values map, simply write down all of the units and strands where one of your values manifests itself. You may wish to include the month or term when the units occur and how often the strands show up. Once you've made your values map, notice what stands out. Do you see patterns in when or how your value manifests itself? What's puzzling or problematic? Now that you've made visible where in your course you can find something you value, you can decide what to add, cut, modify, and rearrange—and what to leave unchanged—in order to serve your values more effectively.

Teachers in a department or team could work together to create a values map and use it to help them make decisions. The eighth-grade teachers who give less group work might consider ways to give more, or they might decide that their students collaborate enough in other classes and need time to think and learn as individuals. The team might decide to spread out the

PROGRAM: **Eighth Grade**

VALUE: **Collaboration**

	Quarter 1	Quarter 2	Quarter 3	Quarter 4	Strands
English	*Bread Givers* trial		*Romeo and Juliet* scene studies		Book partners Peer review of writing
History	Life in Ancient Egypt simulation	Connections to Ancient Rome video		Interviews for "Religion in Our Lives" project	Small group analysis of historical events
Language: Chinese	Farmers' market simulation	Phone conversation roleplay	Cities of China poster project	School emergency videos	Partner conversations Group songs
Language: Spanish	Grammar review board game	Navigating school scavenger hunt	Childhood memories interview project	Cooking shows	Partner conversations Group songs
Math		Graphing systems of equations project			Problem-solving groups Solution-checking pairs
Music					Playing/singing as an ensemble
Physical Education					Working as a team Fair conduct
Science	Bridge project	Making a catapult	Mousetrap car race	Journal article peer review	Lab partnerships

FIGURE 7.1

Values Map for an Eighth-Grade Program

PROGRAM: **Middle School Science**

VALUE: **Sustainability**

Grade 6: Environmental Science	Grade 7: Life Science	Grade 8: Physical Science
Plant Communities (Sept.) • Costs and benefits of different types of roofs • Native vs. non-native plant adaptations Living Systems (Oct.) • Energy flows in food webs • Abiotic factors for survival The Changing Earth (Nov.) • How human factors accelerate weathering and erosion Water as a Resource (May) • Water cycles • How human activities pollute water • How different pollutants affect ecosystems	Characteristics and Needs of Living Things (Oct.) • Need for food, water, and living space Interactions between Living Things and the Environment (May) • How biotic and abiotic factors in an ecosystem affect each other • Carbon cycle • Food web interactions • Symbiosis • Human impact on ecosystems • Renewable and nonrenewable resources • Environmental stewardship	Bridge Project (Oct.) • Designing strong and lasting bridges based on how bridges distribute forces Energy (Apr.) • Types of energy • Loss of energy as heat • Costs and benefits of different energy sources
	Strands: • Protecting yourself and others in the lab • Maintaining lab equipment • Conserving resources and energy in the lab and classroom	

FIGURE 7.2
Values Map for a Middle School Science Program

collaborative work, because some months are full of group projects whereas others have hardly any, or perhaps they'll see reasons to cluster group projects together. A values map helps the team notice areas that need revision and decide what those revisions should entail.

Even if your colleagues won't make or review values maps with you, you can find gaps in your program by mapping it yourself. Though it might feel a little weird to map other people's courses to your values, you can make decisions about your own course based on what you discover in the program. For example, if the eighth-grade history teacher made the map in figure 7.1 (p. 138) herself, she might decide to move her group project about Rome from December, when a lot of group work goes on in other classes, to January, when there isn't any. If your overall program doesn't have *enough* of something you care about, you might be able to put more of it into your course.

Building Programmatic Arcs

If you talk to your colleagues about assignments in your subject or grade, you might discover that your students do similar tasks from class to class. That might be helpful: Grant Wiggins and Jay McTighe (2007) advocate for similar tasks to recur throughout a program, with appropriate increases in the task's sophistication and in the students' expected capabilities. For example, kindergartners might observe and draw bean plants and then spend circle time discussing why some plants have more flowers than others. Though this scene looks very different from goggled tenth graders using a spectrophotometer to measure the concentrations of chemicals in a solution and writing lab reports about their findings, both classes are collecting, displaying, and interpreting data. A cello student might give a recital every year but play increasingly difficult pieces, from "Twinkle, Twinkle, Little Star" to a Brahms sonata, with increasing technical perfection and personal style.

However, similar tasks within a discipline or grade don't always indicate intentional repetition or meaningful progression. Sometimes, two teachers independently think of or find the same idea without realizing it. A popular assignment in middle-grade writing classes is to use the poem "Where I'm From" (Lyon, 1999) as a model for students' own "Where I'm From" poems. You probably can imagine a fifth-grade English teacher asking his students to write "Where I'm From" poems about themselves after his colleague down the hall has asked the very same students to write "Where I'm From" poems about Revolutionary War figures.

Given how easy the internet makes finding assignments, it's not all that unlikely that you and a colleague will come across the same one and want to use it in your respective courses. As teachers of the same subject or grade level, you might read the same magazines, follow the same social media accounts, or subscribe to the same blogs. If you regularly communicate with your colleagues, then instead of accidentally giving the same assignments in multiple courses—or missing opportunities to create meaningful task progressions—you can deliberately give similar or varied assessments within your program.

More generally, even if you don't have the power to change your entire program, starting conversations with your colleagues and administrators can only help you serve your students more effectively. Meanwhile, to borrow an old environmentalist slogan, you can "think globally," in terms of your overall program, and "act locally" by working on your course.

TOOLS FOR USING VALUES TO DESIGN COURSES

We now have seen three ways to transform a course from a heap into a system: create strands to tie it together, diversify tasks to give it balance, and sequence units to provide a sense of meaningful progression—all while attending to the larger programs in which the course is nested. The tools that follow will help you assess how well your course strands, task variety, and unit sequence serve your values so that you can reflect on whether you want to change anything. The game-like *Values Routines* helps you articulate how your class's routines can be opportunities for students to enact important values. In *Assignment Mix*, you'll categorize assignments according to what matters to you, count up how many assignments you've placed in each category, and then decide if the balance feels consistent with your values. *Unit Connections* helps you sequence your units to amplify meaningful themes.

Values Routines

Many teachers include certain learning routines in every unit, or even every lesson. Think of an English class that always begins with five minutes of independent reading, a science class that uses the same set-up procedure for every lab activity, a history class that includes a lesson on analyzing photographs within every unit, or a French class that regularly uses singing to practice grammatical constructions. Some learning routines, such as reviewing the day's agenda or gathering art materials, might be so habitual that you hardly notice you're using them, yet these are still learning events for students. Some learning routines might have names that you've either invented or heard, such as *mindful moments, literature circles* (Daniels, 1994), *exit tickets,* and *problems of the week*; others might not be called anything but are regular, integral parts of your course.

This protocol has you work with a partner or group of colleagues who teach the same course as you do. Together, you'll identify learning routines one or more of you use, and then each of you will associate the routine with values you want your students to enact in your class. Your goal is not to agree upon which routines to use or which values are most important, but rather to explore learning routines together.

You'll write the routines and values on index cards so that you can then flip over pairs of cards at random and describe how the routine can become an opportunity for students to practice behaving in accordance with the value. Using cards introduces a game-like randomness into this process so that you can think more creatively about how learning routines might serve your values. Figure 7.3 (p. 143) shows what it might look like if three colleagues were using this protocol, after they create their cards and set them up to play the game.

To prepare, you need to get a pack of index cards for the group. Each participant will need a pen and a copy of the Examples of Values list from appendix A (p. 187).

Group Protocol

1. As a group, list the learning routines that one or more of you use in your course. Begin each learning routine with an *–ing* verb that names the student's action (such as *reading* independently, *analyzing* historical photographs, or *reviewing* the daily agenda). The following questions might help you identify learning routines in your course.
   - How do you usually begin and end class?
   - What does a typical lesson look like in your classroom?
   - Do you sometimes use certain discussion structures?
   - How do your students take notes or otherwise keep track of their learning?
   - How do your students review the material? Do you regularly use certain games, activities, or strategies?

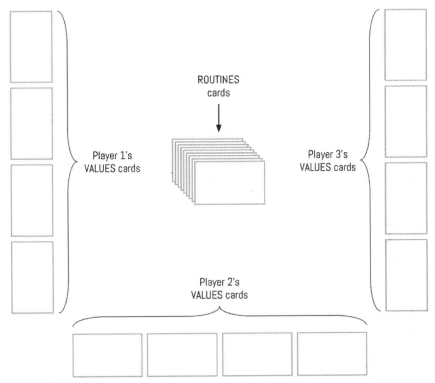

FIGURE 7.3
Setup for a Three-Player Game of Values Routines

- Do you sometimes use certain activities to help students generate ideas?
- Which revision strategies do your students use while working on projects or assignments?
- Do you regularly use reflection activities? What kinds?

2. Write each learning routine on a separate index card, so the group has a single pile of cards, even if not everyone in the group uses all of the learning routines in the pile.

3. Individually, select four values from the Examples of Values list (appendix A, p. 187) that you want your students to practice in your class. Write each value on a separate index card. Each person makes four of their own cards.

4. The group now has a single pile of Routines cards, and each member has four Values cards. Shuffle the Routines cards and place them in a pile,

facedown, in the middle of the table. Shuffle your own Values cards and lay them out facedown in front of you.

5. One group member ("Player 1") flips over a Routines card and a Values card. Player 1 answers the question *How can [Routine] become an opportunity for students to practice [Value]?* For example, if their Routines card said *reading independently* and their Values card said *compassion*, the question they'd answer would be *How can reading independently become an opportunity for students to practice compassion?*

6. Player 1 leaves the Values card faceup to indicate that it's no longer in play.

7. Player 2 can now use the same Routines card that already is faceup or flip over a new Routines card. Player 2 flips over one of their own Values cards and answers the question *How can [Routine] become an opportunity for students to practice [Value]?*

8. This process of describing how a routine can become an opportunity for students to practice a value continues until each player has had four turns and all Values cards are faceup. If you run out of Routines cards before the game ends, just shuffle them, gather them back into a pile, and put the pile facedown in the middle of the table again.

Reflection Questions

- Which question was hardest for you to answer?
- Which answer surprised you most?
- Did you discover any learning routines that you don't currently use but that you want to try?
- Which learning routines seem to offer the most opportunities for your students to enact important values?
- Were there learning routines you wish you'd had a chance to talk about? Which ones? How do they serve some of the values you wrote on your cards?
- Were there learning routines you wish you'd had a chance to hear your colleagues talk about? Which ones? What questions do you have for your colleagues about these learning routines?

Variation

If you're the only person at your school who teaches your course, you can play this game by yourself, but you also can try playing with a colleague who teaches another subject or grade level. Although some learning routines only apply to certain subjects (such as running laps or singing arpeggios), most can apply to any subject. Some learning routines that seem subject-specific might not be; for example, although we might associate independent reading with English class, science students could benefit from beginning class by independently reading science books or articles that they choose for themselves. Playing Values Routines with colleagues who teach other subjects or grade levels could be a fun way to learn more about one another's courses and imagine learning routines for your own course that you haven't tried but that might serve your values.

Assignment Mix

When different kinds of tasks matter to you, you can create a balance among them in your course. You might think of multiple balances you want to create among your course's tasks. Making an assignment mix chart like the one in figure 7.4 (p. 146) can help you see whether you've balanced different kinds of tasks in a way that serves your values.

Figure 7.4 (p. 146) shows an English teacher's assignment mix chart. The chart's column headings represent balances that matter to this particular teacher and that pertain to his discipline. First, he classified the work modalities as written, spoken, or visual. Most of the work is written, but he wants to ensure that his students learn other ways to communicate their ideas. Next, he looked at group sizes and discovered that although his students do most work individually, they occasionally collaborate with a partner or group. Finally, he classified how his students respond to the texts they read in class. Sometimes they write *about* the text, analyzing how it works; sometimes they write *like* the text, in the same genre; and sometimes they enter into a conversation *with* the text by exploring how its themes come up in their own lives. He's created a roughly equal balance of these three ways of using a text to inspire student writing.

Another teacher's assignment mix chart would use different headings. An art teacher like Debbie might consider how many assignments involve certain media or tools. A math teacher might categorize assignments as applicable to students' present lives versus their future lives, or to different domains of life such as physical, financial, and civic well-being. A history teacher might look at whether assignments involve taking a historical actor's perspective or analyzing history from one's own perspective.

For this exercise, you'll create your own assignment mix chart to help you
see what matters to you. Once you make different balances visible, you can
decide how well they serve your values. You can fill out the Assignment Mix
Chart in figure 7.5 (p. 147), or make your own chart and customize the number of columns and rows. After you complete your chart, save it for future

UNIT	ASSIGNMENT	1) Modality	2) Response Type	3) Group Size
Coming-of-Age Stories	Photo essay on what it means to come of age	Visual	With the text	Individuals
	Essay on coming of age in three stories	Written	About the text	Individuals
Poetry with Purpose	Collection of five poems on a single topic	Written	Like the text	Individuals
	Recording for class original poetry playlist	Spoken	Like the text	Individuals
Reinventing Shakespeare: A MIDSUMMER NIGHT'S DREAM	Scene recitation	Spoken	N/A	Partners
	Essay on how setting affects a play's meaning	Written	About the text	Small groups
Defining Success: OF MICE AND MEN	Essay on community definitions of success	Written	With the text	Individuals
	Accompanying artwork	Visual	With the text	Individuals
Redefining Success: THE HOUSE ON MANGO STREET and PERSEPOLIS	Vignette collection	Written	Like the text	Individuals
	Graphic vignette	Visual	Like the text	Individuals
Working for Justice: Activist Memoirs	Essay describing award based on activist	Written	About the text	Individuals
Writing for Justice: A RAISIN IN THE SUN	Dramatic scene about an experience with injustice	Written	Like the text	Partners
TOTALS	Assignments: 12	Written: 7 Spoken: 2 Visual: 3	About: 3 Like: 5 With: 3	Individuals: 9 Partners: 2 Small groups: 1

FIGURE 7.4
An English Teacher's Assignment Mix Chart

reference so you can see how changes you make to a particular unit affect the balance of assignments in your course.

Individual Exercise

1. Fill out the first and second columns of the Assignment Mix Chart (figure 7.5, below) with the names of your units and major assignments you

UNIT	ASSIGNMENT	1)	2)	3)
TOTALS	Assignments:			

FIGURE 7.5
Assignment Mix Chart

give as part of each unit. Decide for yourself which assignments count as *major*. If you give a lot of smaller assignments, you might consider them collectively as a single major assignment. For some units, you might give multiple major assignments.

2. Choose three ways to categorize the assignments, and write them as column headings in your chart beside the *1*, *2*, and *3*. Choose categories from the following list, or come up with your own categories that matter to you.
   - Task format
   - Modality of expression
   - Materials used
   - Tools used
   - Group size
   - Location
   - Voices the work centers
   - Who benefits from the work
   - Whether the work connects to students' own experiences or asks them to consider other people's experiences
   - Whether the task requires students to take another person's perspective or approach the task as themselves

3. Label each assignment within each category. For example, if your category is *group size*, then you might label each assignment *individual*, *partner*, or *small group*.

4. For each category, total up how many assignments have a particular label, and write these totals in the gray boxes at the bottom of their respective columns. If, for example, one of your categories is *group size*, then count the number of individual, partner, and group assignments and write these totals in the gray box at the bottom of the *group size* column.

Reflection Questions
- How did you decide what counts as a major assignment in your course?
- Did any of your totals surprise you?
- Do the balances feel about right, or do you want to give more or fewer assignments in a particular category? If so, how could you adjust some of your current assignments?
- What values does your assignment mix seem to serve? You may wish to consult the Examples of Values in appendix A (p. 187) to help you answer this question.

Variation

Try this exercise with a colleague who teaches the same course as you do. For step 2, agree on which categories you'll both use, and during step 4, compare your totals. What do you notice? You might agree on an ideal assignment mix for your course, but that doesn't have to be your goal. Discussing your respective assignment mixes can simply become a way for you and your colleague to articulate the values you each bring to your course, describe how you balance different types of assignments to serve those values, and notice how students might experience the course as a result.

Unit Connections

If your course follows a textbook or a long-standing tradition, it might be difficult to imagine any other way to sequence it. This exercise is designed to help you rethink your unit sequence in light of your values. First, you'll articulate commonalities between every possible pair of units. Then, you'll rate how connected the units are, as well as how important those connections seem. Finally, you'll consider how you might resequence your units to draw more attention to the important ideas they share.

For the exercise, you'll write about your units and the connections between them on sticky notes. Therefore, you'll need a pack of sticky notes and a pen. Figure 7.6 (p. 150) represents what Ayanna's sticky note table might look like after she finishes doing this exercise with her world geography course. The note at the bottom of a column describes the unit written at the top, and any note in the middle describes connections between the unit at the top of its column and the unit at the beginning of its row.

Your table might be larger or smaller depending on the number of units in your course. If the directions for this exercise seem a bit complicated, keep referring back to the example in figure 7.6 (p. 150) so you can visualize what your table will look like after you complete it.

Individual Exercise

1. Write your unit titles, each on a separate sticky note.
2. Give each unit a letter (*A, B, C,* and so on), just for reference.
3. Put the sticky notes in a row, starting with the one you labeled *A,* across the top of your work surface.
4. Write your unit titles on sticky notes *again,* so that each unit title is written on two different sticky notes. Use the same letters as before to label them.

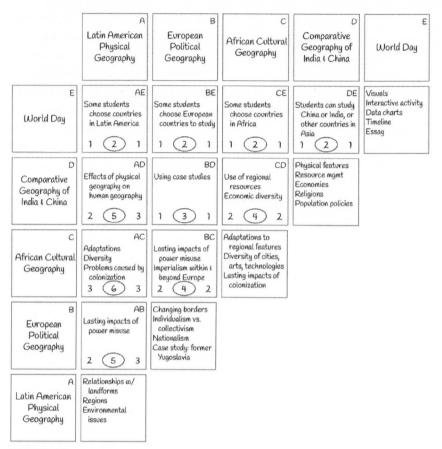

FIGURE 7.6
Connections between World Geography Units

5. Place this second set of sticky notes in a column down the left side of your work surface, in the *opposite* order from the one you used across the top—in reverse alphabetical order, ending with A. Think of each unit title as the heading of a column or row.

6. On a new sticky note, write the most important topics, concepts, skills, or assignments from unit A. You have a small amount of space, so only write a few keywords or phrases. Place the sticky note in column A and row A. Repeat this process for your remaining units.

7. Look at units A and B. Which topics, concepts, skills, or assignments do the two units have in common? These features might or might not be

written among the lists of keywords for their respective units. Write these commonalities on a new sticky note, label it *AB* for reference, and put it on your table at the intersection of units *A* and *B*. Repeat this process until you've identified commonalities between all pairs of units.

8. Looking at *AB*, consider the commonalities you identified between units *A* and *B*. How much do these two units have in common? Rate how connected these two units are, with 3 representing *very connected*, 2 representing *somewhat connected*, and 1 representing *hardly connected*. Put this rating in the lower left-hand corner of sticky note *AB*. Repeat this process for every pair of units (*AC*, *AD*, and so on).

9. Looking again at *AB*, consider how important you think the commonalities between *A* and *B* are, in light of what you wrote about units *A* and *B*. That is, given what you said was important about each individual unit, how important are the topics, concepts, processes, or assignments that the two units share? Rate the importance of these commonalities, with 3 representing *very important*, 2 representing *somewhat important*, and 1 representing *hardly important*. Put this rating in the lower right-hand corner of sticky note *AB*. Repeat this process for every pair of units.

10. You now have two ratings on *AB*. Add these two numbers together, write the total in the bottom center of sticky note *AB*, and circle the number. Repeat this process for every pair of units. Your table is now complete and should look more or less like the example in figure 7.6 (p. 150).

11. Interpret the results. A high total score (5 or 6) means that if you teach those two units consecutively, you can use the commonalities between them to help students gain knowledge you deem important. A low total score (2 or 3) means that it might not make sense to teach these two units consecutively. If a particular unit results in a low total score with all other units, then you may wish to redesign that unit so its content connects to the rest of your course.

Reflection Questions

- Based on this exercise, which units make sense to teach consecutively? Is it possible to rearrange your course so that you can teach those units consecutively?

- Are there units that don't seem connected to any other units? What is the value of teaching this unit's content? Might other ways of teaching this content be a better fit for your overall course?

Extension

After you finish this exercise, photograph your finished table for your records. Then, arrange one set of your unit title sticky notes in a sequence that seems to make sense based on what you learned from doing this exercise. Arrange your other set of unit title sticky notes according to the sequence in which you currently teach them. Discuss with a colleague, or just articulate for yourself, the benefits and drawbacks of each sequence. Even if you don't change the order of your units, noticing the connections between them might help you express those connections more clearly to your students.

ONWARD

This chapter discussed three ways you can make your course function as a system: strands tie the course together so that it feels like a coherent whole, diverse tasks balance different values, and thoughtfully sequenced units create a sense of meaningful progression. We also saw how you can think of your course as nested within larger systems, and how these systems can impact the choices you make for your course. In the next chapter, we'll see how to build meaningful cross-disciplinary connections between your course and others.

8

Use Values to Connect Disciplines

Imagine that it's a Winter Olympics year, and a team of third-grade teachers has been working hard to prepare exciting activities for their students. In social studies, the students are taking a break from learning state geography to do country studies and make flags out of felt. In physical education, they're cutting the distance-running unit to make room for Olympics-like contests such as *mocksled* racing using tied-together scooters. In English, they're competing in a book-o-lympics to see who can read the most before the Games begin. In art, they're painting vases in an Ancient Greek style, with figures playing their favorite sports. In Spanish class, they're learning words related to winter activities, and in math, they're solving word problems about athletes. On the day of opening ceremonies, the third graders will march with their flags into the gym and have a special relay race, and the parents will serve an international potluck at lunch.

Perhaps you've been involved in similar efforts to have students study the same topic, answer the same question, use the same resource, or do the same work across different classes. Such attempts to connect content across disciplines can benefit students in a variety of ways. Presenting the same ideas from multiple angles gives students more opportunities to process information so they can remember and use it (Fogarty, 1991). When we cross disciplines, "the focus for teaching and learning becomes the ideas that can be taken forward and applied in new but related contexts" (Erickson, 1998, pp. 66–67).

Connecting disciplines can also help students develop the capacity for what author Daniel Pink (2006) calls *symphony*, or "seeing the big picture, crossing boundaries, and being able to combine disparate pieces into an arresting new whole" (p. 66)—a key skill now that information is so easy to access. But how can we help our students see the big picture when our different classes create so many little ones? How can we expect students to make unexpected combinations when we build border walls between subjects? Enter cross-disciplinary curriculum.

But just because students learn about the same topic at the same time in multiple classes doesn't mean they'll automatically develop deeper understandings, apply big ideas in novel contexts, or combine unrelated parts into new wholes. Painting in an Ancient Greek style and reading a lot of books might be worthwhile uses of the students' time, but these activities lack the common purpose necessary to engender deeper understandings. It's a heap.

Worse, activities conceived as ways to integrate subjects might take time away from important subject-specific content. Educational psychologist Jere Brophy and education professor Janet Alleman (1991) argue that in integrated units, all activities should be "educationally significant" and "foster, rather than disrupt or nullify, accomplishment of major goals in each subject area" (p. 66). Mocksledding might be fun, but is it more educationally significant than the running unit it displaces? In social studies, the country reports disrupt the regularly scheduled curriculum, and whether making flags fosters the accomplishment of major learning goals in history seems questionable.

At the same time, let's not dismiss the teachers' efforts. They came up with creative ideas, worked hard to craft a unit they only teach once every four years, care about engaging their students, and seem willing to collaborate. If they could come together around a topic, perhaps together they could also make the unit more meaningful.

Let's return to the Donella Meadows (2008) definition of a system: "an interconnected set of elements that is coherently organized in a way that achieves something" (p. 11). For the Olympics unit to become a system, its elements would need to work together to achieve some purpose. What makes the Olympics worth studying in third grade? Perhaps the key understanding is that people from all over the world share an experience through the Olympics, and the essential question could be *What brings people together?* Or maybe what's important is that great athletes work hard to improve, and the inquiry could be *Why should I work to get better at something when I'm already good at it?* Or maybe the fact that the Olympics have endured for so long matters: *What makes a tradition survive?*

Once the teachers understand the unit's purpose, each of them can craft lessons to fit that purpose—and that fit into their curriculum instead of feeling like a detour. The teachers would need to explain to the students how the lessons relate to the unit's purpose and to material they're learning in other classes. By identifying and sticking to a commonly valued purpose, teachers can make their students' experience more meaningful and coherent, instead of subverting that aim by creating a new heap of unrelated lessons. This chapter offers ways to do that.

DECIDING WHETHER TO CONNECT DISCIPLINES

In categorizing ways to connect curriculum across subjects, interdisciplinary studies professor William Newell (2013) identifies two key distinctions. First, teachers of different subjects might or might not *cooperate*; they might operate together by having their students learn about the same topic, read the same book, or work on the same project—or they might operate separately and teach about different things in their different classes. Second, even if teachers of different subjects *cooperate*, they might or might not *coordinate* their efforts toward a single purpose (Newell, 2013). That is, even when teachers share a common *what*, they might not share a common *why*.

When teachers have all different *whats*, we might call their approach *unidisciplinary*: everyone does their own thing, in their own discipline. When teachers have a common *what* but not a common *why*, we might call their approach *multidisciplinary*. The Olympics study is multidisciplinary because the teachers are sharing a topic, but they're teaching about it in different ways and for different purposes. When teachers have a common *what* and a common *why*, working together toward a single shared purpose, we might call that approach *interdisciplinary*.

Even though we usually think of cooperation and coordination as good things, an interdisciplinary approach is not necessarily better than one that's multidisciplinary or unidisciplinary. All of the previous chapters in this book contain examples of meaningful unidisciplinary units. In your course, you teach important content for important purposes. As helpful as connecting to other courses might be, it has a cost. Our time with students is limited, and any time we spend on multidisciplinary or interdisciplinary studies will come from somewhere. How do we know if that time is worthwhile, or if that time would be better spent on the meaningful unidisciplinary learning experiences we already planned for our classes?

When deciding whether to create curriculum that connects disciplines, we can ask two values questions, based on the two distinctions Newell (2013) identified:

1. Is the potential shared content more important than the course-specific content it would replace?
2. Is there a shared goal that's more important than the goals in each course?

If you answer *yes* to the first question but *no* to the second, consider creating a multidisciplinary unit, in which you and one or more of your colleagues teach the same content for your own important purposes. If you answer *yes* to both questions, consider creating an interdisciplinary unit, in which you and one or more of your colleagues teach the same content for a shared important purpose. And if you can't honestly answer *yes* to either question, then you probably created a meaningful, values-consistent unidisciplinary unit that isn't worth replacing. Any of these outcomes is a good one.

In previous chapters, we saw how to use inquiries, rehearsals, and projects to focus units. We might now imagine unidisciplinary, multidisciplinary, and interdisciplinary approaches to inquiries, rehearsals, and projects, which would give us nine possible unit types! But instead of discussing all nine possibilities, we'll consider two that work especially well: interdisciplinary inquiries and multidisciplinary projects.

INTERDISCIPLINARY INQUIRIES

Inquiries, by their nature, tend to be interdisciplinary even when they take place in one class. We ask an important question and go wherever the question leads. In a collaborative interdisciplinary inquiry, teachers of different subjects contribute resources, tools, methodologies, and perspectives from their respective disciplines.

An interdisciplinary essential question directs attention to something that multiple learning communities find important, elicits thinking that integrates multiple approaches, and piques the students' curiosity about a larger problem or idea. The following examples show what interdisciplinary essential questions sound like.

- How does structure relate to function?
- How do codes work? What can we do if we know the code?
- How does success relate to setting, and what can we do to become more successful in our setting?
- How does technology both help and hinder us?
- What does it mean to be a critical consumer—whether of goods, services, information, or ideas?
- What does sustainable eating look like—personally, culturally, economically, socially, and ecologically?
- When is a traditional approach best, when is newer better, and how do we know?
- How does diversity ensure a thriving and resilient community?
- How can a small change have big consequences?
- When are rules helpful and when do they get in the way?
- How can sequences affect outcomes?

If you and a group of colleagues try to write an essential interdisciplinary question, you might not come up with one that feels right for everyone—or every subject. Even topics that might lend themselves to meaningful interdisciplinary study won't necessarily work with the specific curriculum in your grade level. A fourth-grade team that wants to create an interdisciplinary inquiry about democracy might find connections to math, but maybe not the math that their fourth graders learn. If some teachers or subjects can't connect to the question, consider finding a different one or having only the courses with an authentic connection participate.

Designing Interdisciplinary Essential Questions

Imagine that a group of fifth-grade teachers discovers the theme of *change* coming up in every single subject. They are excited about this theme because everything in their students' lives is on the cusp of change: their bodies, their social groups, and even their school as they prepare to leave elementary and go to middle. The fifth-grade team comes up with the essential question *How do things change?* Then, the teachers meet again to discuss how to use the question to focus a unit.

The English teacher says her class can study how a character changes in any book they read. The history teacher says his students can examine changes in American society that led to or resulted from any of the events they study, and the science teacher says she spends the entire year teaching about changes in plants, bodies of water, and biomes. In math, the students can look at how changes in numerical patterns affect the shape of corresponding graphs, and in both physical education and music, the students can examine how small changes to form affect the quality of their performance.

Interdisciplinary themes are the biggies that recur throughout history. It's no surprise, then, if these themes pop up in all of the courses in your grade level—if not every grade level. Remember that one purpose of essential questions is to help teachers decide what to include in the unit and what to leave out. A question won't serve that purpose if it's so broad that anything potentially can go into the unit. A broad question also presents the danger of reductionism: a changing biome might have something in common with a musician making changes to her form, but they're not the same.

One way to deal with a too-broad question is to discuss why the theme is important for students to consider and write a more specific question that suggests that important idea. Because the fifth-grade teachers are drawn to the theme of change because their students' lives are changing, they could use the question *How does one change lead to more changes?* or *What are the best ways to respond to change?* Other questions about change with more unit-focusing potential could be *How do we know if a change is for the better?* or *How can we predict the outcome of a change?* or *What makes people want to change?*

If an essential question contains a general or vague term, such as *change*, choosing a more specific term can help focus the unit. Depending on what the fifth-grade teachers think is most important, they could use a term such as *ripple effect* or *adaptation* in their question. Students are more likely to notice a more specific term like *adaptation* when it appears in different classes than a more general term like *change*.

If an inquiry takes place in multiple classrooms with multiple teachers, the students might not even realize that the material is all part of one unit, or notice interconnections between lessons, unless teachers make these explicit. Teachers using an interdisciplinary essential question can post it in all of the classrooms, put it on all of the unit materials, and give students frequent opportunities to work with it in discussions, games, writing assignments, or other activities.

Using Interdisciplinary Essential Questions across Courses

An interdisciplinary question focuses your students on important connections among multiple subjects. But the question won't tell you how your discipline's content and tools contribute meaningfully to the inquiry. That's why you can create a discipline-specific subsidiary question of the overarching essential interdisciplinary question and use it to focus your portion of the inquiry. Figures 8.1 (p. 160) and 8.2 (p. 161) show examples of interdisciplinary questions along with discipline-specific subsidiary questions that teachers could use in their classes.

In the first example (figure 8.1, p. 160), the questions all use the word *code*. Hearing this same word echo through the questions in different classes helps students understand how these inquiries interrelate and contribute to a single, larger unit. In the second example (figure 8.2, p. 161), the questions all have different language that relates to their respective disciplines. If teachers use these discipline-specific questions in their different classes, then they should explicitly and frequently refer to the overarching question *How does structure relate to function?* so that students can see how the various smaller inquiries contribute to a larger whole.

That larger whole is the essence of interdisciplinary study. According to Newell and his colleague William Green (1982), students should use each discipline's concepts, methodologies, and theories when engaging in an inquiry, and then integrate insights from various disciplines "by reconciling them if they are inconsistent, or combining them into a larger whole if they are consistent" (p. 25). In studying how members of an ancient society, literary characters, modern language speakers, musicians, mathematicians, and our own biological processes use codes, students might derive larger insights—such as that we can use codes to access the benefits of our surroundings, or that codes indicate who is and isn't in a group. They might reconcile inconsistencies, such as by discussing how biological organisms don't know the codes in their DNA in the same way people know cultural codes, and that the way we learn the codes of our home cultures might be more implicit than the way we learn the codes of a new place or practice. Noticing such connections and distinc-

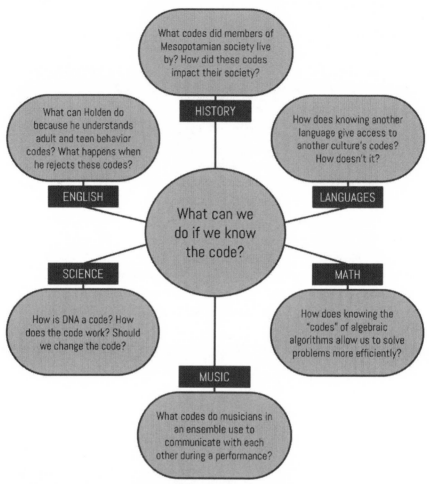

FIGURE 8.1
Interdisciplinary and Subsidiary Questions for a Unit on Codes

tions doesn't only help students understand codes more fully; it also helps them practice both critical and generative thinking.

Although some students might reach these kinds of insights on their own, others might not make the necessary connections without prompting, and some might not even recognize the interdisciplinary inquiry as such because they're so used to thinking about each subject on its own terms and within the four walls of a particular classroom. To ensure that all students integrate their

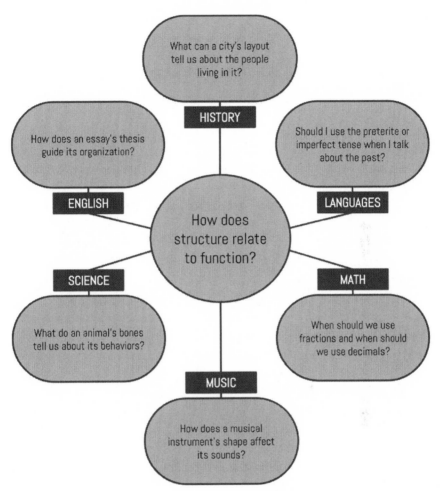

FIGURE 8.2
Interdisciplinary and Subsidiary Questions for a Unit on Structure

discoveries, ask them to consider content from your class and others. To do *that*, you need to talk to your colleagues frequently, not just to plan the unit but while teaching it. That way, you all can refer to each other's content with your own students and help them discover meaningful similarities and differences.

Students don't necessarily have to create a big presentation, paper, or display showing their integrated insights. Synthesizing their understandings can be as simple as having discussions in their different classes. In some ways, a more informal and ongoing series of discussions better parallels how inter-disciplinary inquiries unfold in the real world. Larger questions don't have answers; they stir reflection, experimentation, debate, storytelling, imagining, and further questioning. Rather than having a tangible outcome, you can let the process itself be the outcome.

Simultaneous and Serial Inquiries

A *unit*, again, is a time-bound study of a particular topic. Many interdisci-plinary units are time bound in that students learn about a concept simulta-neously in different classes. Perhaps for several weeks in October, students go from class to class and learn about codes, whether in DNA or Mesopotamian society or an algebra problem or a jazz ensemble. Though students might be more likely to connect ideas presented at around the same time, those who enjoy learning different things in different classes—or who don't find codes all that exciting—are just waiting for October to end.

As an alternative to the simultaneous inquiry, consider a serial inquiry that takes place in one course at a time. A serial interdisciplinary inquiry begins in one class, looking like a regular old unidisciplinary unit in that subject. Over time, though, the inquiry appears in a second class, and perhaps even a third and a fourth. Figure 8.3 (p. 163) has a diagram showing how an inquiry can move from class to class over a period of several months.

In a serial inquiry, instead of thinking about a concept in different classes simultaneously, students examine it in one class at a time, incorporating new knowledge and skills that help them move forward into something more advanced—like how a snowball rolling down a hill gathers in size and momentum. Students have time to develop an increasingly sophisticated un-derstanding of the concept. They also are less likely to get bored if they're not bombarded with the same topic in every class at once.

MULTIDISCIPLINARY PROJECTS

Projects, by their nature, lend themselves to a multidisciplinary approach. Unlike the relatively simple tasks that help students rehearse discrete skills, projects are complex undertakings that usually involve skills beyond any given discipline. When Xiomara asks her students to collect, display, and dis-cuss data about functional relationships in their lives, the project takes place only during math class, but the skills involved—describing their findings

How does success relate to setting, and what can we do to become more successful in our setting?

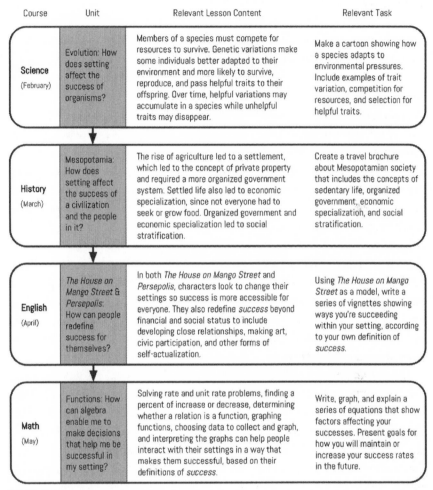

Course	Unit	Relevant Lesson Content	Relevant Task
Science (February)	Evolution: How does setting affect the success of organisms?	Members of a species must compete for resources to survive. Genetic variations make some individuals better adapted to their environment and more likely to survive, reproduce, and pass helpful traits to their offspring. Over time, helpful variations may accumulate in a species while unhelpful traits may disappear.	Make a cartoon showing how a species adapts to environmental pressures. Include examples of trait variation, competition for resources, and selection for helpful traits.
History (March)	Mesopotamia: How does setting affect the success of a civilization and the people in it?	The rise of agriculture led to a settlement, which led to the concept of private property and required a more organized government system. Settled life also led to economic specialization, since not everyone had to seek or grow food. Organized government and economic specialization led to social stratification.	Create a travel brochure about Mesopotamian society that includes the concepts of sedentary life, organized government, economic specialization, and social stratification.
English (April)	The House on Mango Street & Persepolis: How can people redefine success for themselves?	In both *The House on Mango Street* and *Persepolis*, characters look to change their settings so success is more accessible for everyone. They also redefine *success* beyond financial and social status to include developing close relationships, making art, civic participation, and other forms of self-actualization.	Using *The House on Mango Street* as a model, write a series of vignettes showing ways you're succeeding within your setting, according to your own definition of *success*.
Math (May)	Functions: How can algebra enable me to make decisions that help me be successful in my setting?	Solving rate and unit rate problems, finding a percent of increase or decrease, determining whether a relation is a function, graphing functions, choosing data to collect and graph, and interpreting the graphs can help people interact with their settings in a way that makes them successful, based on their definitions of *success*.	Write, graph, and explain a series of equations that show factors affecting your successes. Present goals for how you will maintain or increase your success rates in the future.

FIGURE 8.3
Serial Interdisciplinary Unit on Success

graphically, algebraically, and verbally to their classmates; making an eye-catching and awareness-raising mini-poster—come from within and beyond math. Of course, Xiomara can assign this project on her own and should feel confident teaching visual and verbal communication in math class, but we might think of ways her colleagues in the arts and English departments could contribute—perhaps just by giving Xiomara advice and resources, or perhaps by having students do some of the work as part of their courses.

With your colleagues, you can design multidisciplinary projects that leverage each teacher's expertise and fulfill important objectives in each course. Let's imagine that in a history class, students examine the Civil War from various perspectives. They read accounts from eyewitnesses who are diverse in terms of geographic location, national origin, race, gender, socioeconomic status, and occupation. Meanwhile, in their English class, these students read the novel *Same Sun Here* (House & Vaswani, 2012), which is written in letters between an Indian American girl living in New York City and a white boy living in rural Kentucky. While reading, the students analyze how the imagery conveys each character's voice and setting, and they discuss the book's themes of finding common ground, building an authentic relationship, and persisting through struggle.

The English and history teachers decide to create a single project for their unit. Each student writes a story set during the Civil War, written as a series of letters between two characters who have very different perspectives. The English teacher evaluates the story's imagery, characterization, and editing, whereas the history teacher evaluates how accurately it conveys historical details, perspectives, and events. Figure 8.4 (p. 165) shows the rubric they use to assess their students' work. It articulates a single task for the students to complete while also designating elements each teacher will evaluate.

If you assign a multidisciplinary project, you and your colleagues need to decide how you'll assess the students' work. You might come up with separate grades on your own or one grade together. You might work as a team to write guidelines, or you might each contribute separate criteria to a single rubric. There isn't a right way; you and your colleagues need to find an approach that serves everyone's values. If you can't, then you're better off creating separate tasks for your courses.

Organizing a Multidisciplinary Project

A multidisciplinary task will be complex, so the students likely will need more support, but they will benefit from the challenge. Doing one task for multiple subjects allows students to consolidate their understandings and put more effort into producing a single excellent piece of work. The students also will benefit from multiple teachers' and classmates' feedback—as long as

Units: Perspectives on the Civil War (History) and Reading *Same Sun Here* (English)

Assignment: Story in Letters

Using *Same Sun Here* as a model, and drawing upon your knowledge of the Civil War era, write a series of letters between two fictional characters who would have had very different perspectives on the Civil War.

Your HISTORY teacher will look for the following elements:	BASIC	EFFECTIVE	EXEMPLARY
Accurate historical details give a sense of what life was like during the Civil War.			
At least three key Civil War figures or events are included in the story, and the characters indicate what each figure or event means to them.			
The overall story reflects a strong understanding of how different people viewed the Civil War differently.			
Your ENGLISH teacher will look for the following elements:	BASIC	EFFECTIVE	EXEMPLARY
Specific, detailed images help the reader vividly imagine each narrator's setting.			
Vocabulary and poetic devices give each character a distinct voice.			
The entire story is edited to make it easy to read: it has a title, letters are dated and have greetings and closings, and there are no errors in capitalization, punctuation, spelling, or grammar.			

FIGURE 8.4
Example Rubric for a Multidisciplinary Project

each teacher devotes class time for everyone to create and refine their work product, share it with one another, and develop the knowledge they'll need.

It's hard even in one class to make sure you teach all of the skills students need to do well on a complex task—especially skills associated with the task but not your discipline. A Spanish teacher might not assign a video project just for his class because teaching how to use cameras and editing software would take away too much time from speaking the language, but he might be willing to teach *some* videography skills if his colleagues pick up the rest in their classes.

In a multidisciplinary project, there are more potential experts who can teach skills like these, and no one teacher needs to devote as much class time to them.

On the other hand, the diffused responsibility for teaching skills that don't relate to anyone's subject means it's possible *no one* will teach them, and the whole team might be frustrated or blame each other when the students' work is subpar. As a team, decide who teaches what, in what order, and for how long so that everyone allocates instructional and preparation time fairly.

To ensure that everyone understands their responsibilities and time frames, make a project calendar that works for each individual class and for the unit as a whole—but build in flexibility. What if someone doesn't finish a lesson that's supposed to lead into an activity in another class? What if someone finds a new resource? What if a student asks a question no one expected? Including an extra work day in each class leaves room for adjustments, and checking in daily keeps everyone informed of changes.

Multidisciplinary Upcycling

As we saw in the previous chapter, *upcycling* involves using work product students have already created as raw materials for a new piece of work. If you think creatively with your colleagues, you might find opportunities for students to use something they produce in one class as raw materials to upcycle in another class. For example, students could grow vegetables as part of a science unit on plant development and use the vegetables when they do cooking demonstrations as part of a unit on command-form verbs in a language class. They could upcycle graphs from a math class into collages in art. They could write essays in history and choreograph them in dance.

Upcycling work from class to class doesn't require the teachers involved to share the same goals. If a student creates a video for physical education to display her progress in softball, she fulfills the task's purpose when she makes and presents the video. Later, in science class, this student might add equations and commentary to her video to describe the motion of the ball during different at bats. The physical education and science teachers have very different goals in their respective courses, but together they can create an opportunity for the student to upcycle her work product from one class to another.

Upcycling also can help teachers overcome some logistical barriers of multidisciplinary projects. Imagine that when Lily, a high-school drama teacher, tells her ninth graders that they'll perform various types of scenes, she learns that they'll *write* scenes in their English class that spring. Lily meets with Sunil, one of the ninth-grade English teachers. He says his students write the scenes after reading *The Laramie Project* (Kaufman, 2014) but don't perform them because that would take away too much time from other reading and writing units. Both teachers like the idea of having their students work on their original scenes in English *and* drama class so they'll more deeply understand how playwrights and actors contribute to a play's meaning.

As they discuss logistics, the two teachers realize that because ninth-grade performing arts courses are on a rotating schedule where Lily sees a third of the students each trimester, only those who see her in the spring term would be able to work on their dramatic scenes in her class. They also realize that while Sunil's students write scenes, the other ninth-grade English teachers assign essays about the play—but Lily's drama classes have students from all different English classes mixed together.

At schools that prioritize discipline-based classes in the schedule—not to mention in the budget—teachers of different subjects can't necessarily work with a single group of students at the same time. But they can use their work product from one class as raw material for a new project in another.

Because Lily teaches tenth grade, too, she decides that after her students write scenes as ninth graders with Sunil, they can perform them as tenth graders with her. Even though the scenes will be finished as far as Sunil is concerned, they'll provide the raw material for a new project in Lily's class. The students who didn't write scenes in ninth grade can still perform in their peers' scenes or serve as directors. Finally, even though Lily's course focuses on acting, nothing is stopping the students from revising their writing. In fact, as actors, they might discover clunky bits of dialogue and awkward transitions that they can then change. Multidisciplinary upcycling gives students an opportunity to see their own work in new ways and to enrich their skills in multiple fields.

What do your students create in their other classes, during the year when you teach them and in their previous years at school? How might you use these work products as starting points for new projects in your class? How could a multidisciplinary project become an opportunity for students to see connections across disciplines, develop their skills, and find new meaning in their work?

GETTING COLLEAGUES INTERESTED IN CROSSING DISCIPLINES

Imagine that Luisa's sixth-grade science classes do an intensive study of freshwater biomes, beginning with a field trip to a lake. While chaperoning this trip, the social studies teacher, Jae, learns that the fisheries in the lake have been depleted over the years. On the bus back, Jae and Luisa talk about a possible multidisciplinary project. The students learn about the ecological factors leading to the depleted fisheries in science class in October. In social studies, their November unit is on government, and they learn about how laws get made. Jae and Luisa want to have the sixth graders write letters to their local legislature asking for stronger protections for fish.

As Luisa and Jae get more excited about their unit, they start talking about how other colleagues could get involved. "In music, Brandon could have them write songs to raise awareness about the fisheries," Luisa says. "Ooh— and in math, Tova could do something with depletion rates."

Excitement about a new project can be contagious, but it also can be alienating to colleagues who didn't participate in creating the idea. Not everyone in a group will share the same values, prioritize their values in the same way, or want to serve those values with the same project. Brandon might want his students to appreciate music as music, not as a means of persuasion. Even if Tova is an environmental activist and loves that her students are doing the fish unit in other classes, a study of depletion rates might not fit into her math curriculum.

Instead of trying to convince others to buy into an idea, we can talk about the values it serves. Luisa and Jae want their students to understand connections between themselves and their surroundings and to take action in the community. If they hope more teachers on their team will join in the fishery fun, Luisa and Jae could talk about the values that inspired them to want to do this project and how the project will move them toward these values. Then, they can invite their colleagues to participate in the unit—and might be surprised by creative ways their colleagues think to connect in.

If no one else is interested, then Luisa and Jae can still proceed on their own, report back to their colleagues about their progress, and solicit their help in solving problems that inevitably arise. Eventually, Brandon and Tova might want to be part of the unit, or they might not, but at least they won't feel shut out.

MULTIDISCIPLINARY LEARNING EVENTS WITHIN UNIDISCIPLINARY UNITS

Connections between courses don't have to be big to be effective. If interdisciplinary inquiries and multidisciplinary projects sound like too much to take on, try creating one learning event that crosses disciplines. A single field trip to a glassblowing museum could serve as a foundational experience for a chemistry unit on states of matter and an art unit on outdoor installations. Students could read *The Immortal Life of Henrietta Lacks* (Skloot, 2017) as part of a biology unit on genetics and a history unit on resisting oppression. They could use Groove Pizza (NYU Music Experience Design Lab, 2017)—an app that allows users to inscribe different geometric shapes within a circle, which turns to produce beats that correspond to the shapes—to study both geometry in math class and rhythm in music class.

One discipline-spanning learning event—a shared lesson, assignment, speaker, text, performance, field trip, or service project—allows students to refer back to this common experience as the units go forward. Find out what your colleagues include in their courses and imagine how that same learning experience, resource, or task could fit into your course and serve a purpose you value. Smaller connections might spark ideas for bigger ones. But even if they don't, they provide occasions for you and your colleagues to talk about your values and see where they overlap.

Connecting disciplines even in small ways requires time—to share, ask questions, plan, and learn new material—and the outcome probably won't be perfect the first year, and maybe not the second or third year either. But the biggest barriers to crossing disciplines can be our own thoughts and feelings. *It's too hard. There's too much to think about. I don't know where to begin. It won't work. I'll just wait. My course is fine. The students are happy. Let's not rock the boat. It wasn't that great an idea anyway.*

Crossing disciplines creates potential conflict, logistical hurdles, and the effort of learning new content and designing new experiences for your students. Sticking to your own discipline is almost always easier and more comfortable. At the same time, struggling together to create something meaningful can strengthen your relationships with your colleagues. As a team, you can decide that crossing disciplines is too complicated and not worth the effort, or you can help each other overcome internal barriers and hold each other accountable—not to a set of standards created by people you've never met or to an administrative initiative, but to your values as teachers.

TOOLS FOR USING VALUES TO CONNECT DISCIPLINES

Most academic standards and programs are discipline based, particularly after the elementary grades, and often there, too. Even when students stay in the same classroom with the same teacher, they often learn in periods or blocks of discipline-based study. Creating units is enough of a challenge when you have a topic, text, or project from which to proceed. Crossing disciplines often means starting from scratch. It also often means working with colleagues who teach other courses, which might lead to exciting ideas but also might lead to conflict and resentment, or just wasted time, if you don't have a process that elicits and honors everyone's contributions.

The tools in this chapter create inclusive ways for you and your colleagues to explore ideas for crossing disciplines, based on your values. *Finding What's Essential across Disciplines* is a version of the *Finding What's Essential* protocol from chapter 4 but designed for teams of teachers to create meaningful interdisciplinary inquiries. *Assignment Mashup* has you and a colleague create possible multidisciplinary projects out of existing assignments in your respective courses. *Participation Invitation* is a way to share an idea for crossing disciplines with your colleagues when you aren't sure that they'll be as invested in it as you are.

Finding What's Essential across Disciplines

In any inquiry-based unit, an essential question directs attention to what's most important about the content, elicits higher-order thinking, and piques students' curiosity. In an interdisciplinary inquiry, an essential question helps teachers and students stay focused on what matters across courses, synthesize understandings, and ask their own questions. If the question doesn't feel meaningful to everyone, it won't serve those purposes.

Before you can write an interdisciplinary essential question, you'll need a topic for your unit. If you don't have a topic already, look for one in your community, your students' lives, current events, or something you encounter. You could study an event, such as the Olympics, in multiple ways. You could use a single resource—a book, film, speaker, or field trip—in multiple classes. You could choose an issue, such as sexual harassment or mountaintop removal, to study through multiple lenses. You could use a skill, such as taking notes or public speaking, or a theme, such as success or democracy. Ideas for interdisciplinary units can come from just about anywhere.

Once you have a topic, you and a group of colleagues who teach different disciplines will come together to generate a question to use across your courses. If each team member teaches multiple subjects (as many elementary teachers do), then each person can consider the topic from the perspective of one discipline. You'll respond to prompts that help each of you articulate what matters about a topic, and then work together to phrase what you each find important as questions. You'll then choose one question that suggests a path for teaching and learning in each subject and that reflects your collective values.

Group Protocol

1. Identify a topic for the group to consider for interdisciplinary study.
2. Individually, all members of the group write in response to one or more of the prompts below, filling in the blanks with the identified topic. You don't have to go in any particular order or respond to all of the prompts. Write until you get bored or stuck. Then, switch prompts. Spend about ten minutes writing, trying your best not to stop. If you start to make any judgments, positive or negative, about the quality of your writing or ideas, just notice these thoughts and turn your attention back to responding.
   - What don't I know about ___?
   - What would a person we study in our class—a historical figure, literary character, artist, composer, athlete, scientist, or mathematician—have to say about ___?
   - Which skills are my students currently working on in my class? How might the skills help them make sense of ___ or some aspect of it?
   - Which topic will my students learn about next in my course? How is this topic connected to ___?
   - How did I learn about ___? What about those learning experiences could I bring to my classroom, and what would not be appropriate for my students or subject?
   - If a workshop about ___ were at a conference for practitioners of my discipline, what might the workshop's title be, and what would happen in it?

3. Each person takes a turn sharing what they wrote—all of it, or at least a substantial portion. While listening, everyone else takes notes on anything striking that each person says.

4. Once each person has shared, everyone takes a few moments to review their notes and look for connections and commonalities among the responses.

5. Group members say back connections and commonalities, but framed as questions. Try to generate different questions, or different versions of the same question. A scribe writes down the questions.

6. The group discusses which questions seem to have the most potential to shape an inquiry across courses. At this point, any group member can offer suggestions for rewording the questions or ideas for how they'd approach the unit.

Reflection Questions

- Did you discover anything interesting about the topic? Your course? Your colleagues? Yourself?
- If the group chose an interdisciplinary question, what would be a subject-specific version for your class?
- Was there a question the group seemed *not* to find useful but that you want to think more about? How could that questions shape an inquiry in your class, regardless of whether the group uses it?
- How willing are you to do interdisciplinary work in your class? Why aren't you *less* willing? What would make you *more* willing?
- What would a failed interdisciplinary inquiry look like? What steps can you take to make these failures less likely?
- Even if the unit does fail, why would your efforts to conceive of, plan, and implement the unit still be worthwhile?

Extension

Coming up with an interdisciplinary essential question is challenging, and it's only a beginning. You and your team still need to decide whether to conduct this inquiry simultaneously or serially, and each of you needs to design meaningful subject-specific learning tasks. If you create a good essential question, schedule regular follow-up meetings to discuss the unit's content and logistics.

Assignment Mashup

Although most projects involve skills and knowledge from multiple disciplines, that doesn't mean you and your colleagues will easily find projects that authentically fit into both courses. For this protocol, *Assignment Mashup*, you and a colleague who teaches a different subject will use existing assignments from each of your courses to help you come up with a multidisciplinary project that fits into both. The protocol gets its name—and its inspiration—from the practice of combining the vocal track from one pop song with the instrumentation from another, resulting in a new song that reflects yet transcends both of the originals. You and your colleague will need a copy of the Mashup Chart (figure 8.5, p. 174) to fill out together.

Figure 8.6 (p. 175) shows a example mashup chart that an English teacher and an engineering teacher filled out, using assignments from their respective courses. In English class, students read *Akata Witch* (Okorafor, 2017), a fantasy book in which the main character feels caught between identifiers—American and Nigerian, black and albino, soccer-loving and sun-sensitive—until she discovers her magical abilities, learns to control them, and befriends others who have powers. During the unit, students analyze how fantasy stories can communicate truths about the real world, even as they depend on magic. Then, students write their own fantasy stories based on learning experiences from their own lives.

Meanwhile, in their engineering class, these same students learn about designer Rob Tieben, whose installations encourage teens to engage in social play (Tieben et al., 2014). For example, Tieben's group designed a camera that captured kids' movements and projected cartoonified versions on a screen, which got them to move in funny ways, and another installation set up two seats such that one kid's movements on one seat made the other seat tilt or vibrate (Tieben et al., 2014). The engineering teacher showed his students Tieben's work and then challenged them to engineer ways to encourage play, creativity, and interaction in common spaces around the school.

For the protocol, the two teachers wrote out their original assignments and identified three keywords or phrases in each one. Then, they used different combinations of keywords in new assignments that they wrote in their chart (figure 8.6, p. 175). After brainstorming, they can decide together if any of these multidisciplinary projects fits into one or both of their courses.

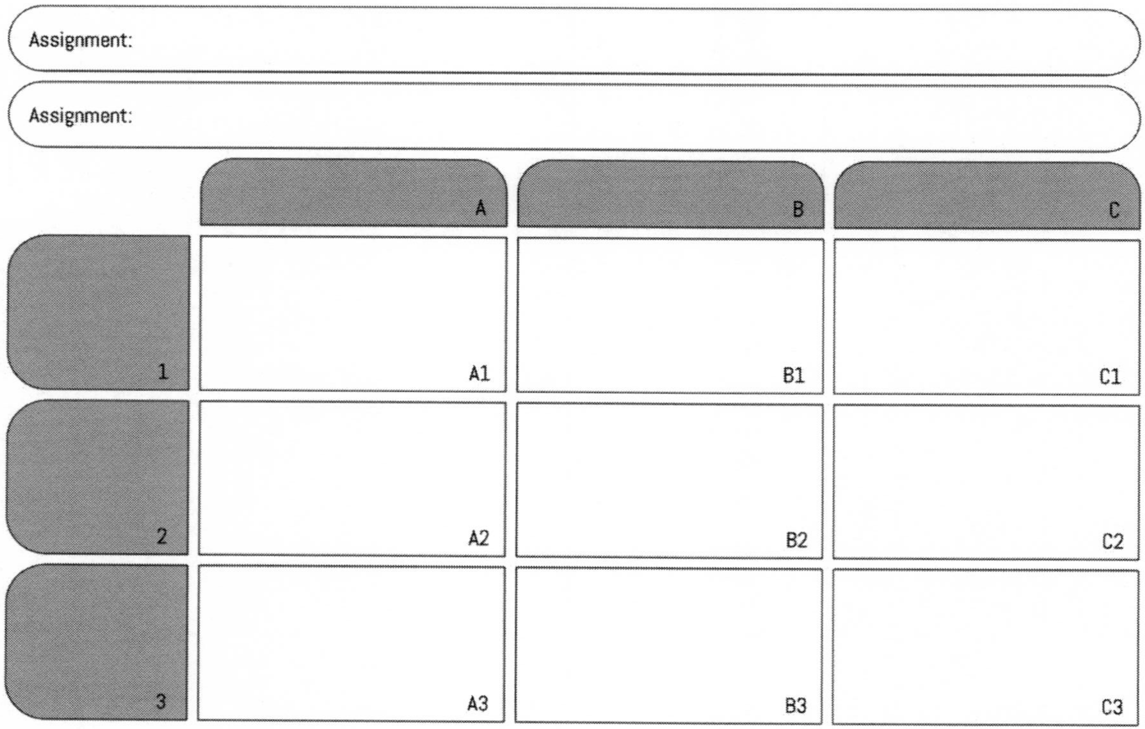

Assignment:

Assignment:

	A	B	C
1	A1	B1	C1
2	A2	B2	C2
3	A3	B3	C3

FIGURE 8.5
Mashup Chart

Assignment: *Write a fantasy story based on a specific learning experience from your life.*

Assignment: *Design an installation that encourages creative or playful interaction in a common space at school.*

	fantasy story A	**learning experience** B	**your life** C
installation 1	Design an installation inspired by a fantasy story. A1	Create an installation based upon a learning experience you had in the past. B1	Design and installation based on a significant person, place, or moment in your life. C1
creative or playful interaction 2	Write a fantasy story that encourages creative or playful interaction between the reader and the text. A2	Design a way for your peers to learn about themselves or each other through creative or playful interaction. B2	Write an essay about a time when you had a creative or playful interaction with someone in your life. C2
common space 3	Write a fantasy story set in a common space at school. A3	Redesign a common space to promote more positive learning experiences for those who use it. B3	Write an essay that compares and contrasts how you've related to three different common spaces you've encountered in your life. C3

FIGURE 8.6
Mashups of an English and an Engineering Assignment

Partner Protocol

1. Get together with a colleague who teaches a different subject from yours but in the same grade level. You need one copy of the Mashup Chart (figure 8.5, p. 174) to share.

2. Individually, each of you chooses a project you already give in your class. You may wish to first list all of your course's projects, then choose one that you think is interesting or important, or that you just want to explore further.

3. On your chart, write each assignment in a sentence or two, as if you're articulating it for students. Do this step individually, so that each of you uses your own words to write your assignment.

4. Individually, identify three keywords or phrases from your own assignment.

5. Write the three keywords or phrases from one subject's assignment in areas *A*, *B*, and *C* across the top of the chart, and write the three keywords or phrases from the other subject's assignment in areas *1*, *2*, and *3* down the left-hand column of the chart.

6. Begin with keywords *A* and *1*. Together, make up an assignment that uses these keywords, articulating the assignment in no more than a sentence or two. Write this assignment in box *A1*. Continue by making up an assignment that uses keywords *A* and *2*, and then *A* and *3*, and so on, until you've written nine different assignments. Work quickly; the goal at this stage is to fill all nine boxes in no more than fifteen minutes. Don't worry about whether you think the assignment would work—in either of your courses, or at all. If you come up with two ideas for the same box, decide which one to write down, or write both. If you can't come up with anything for a particular box, skip it and move on. If you have empty boxes after working for fifteen minutes, that's fine.

7. Discuss which (if any) assignments you'd consider giving in your courses. Some assignments might not work for either course. Others might make sense as multidisciplinary projects that students would work on in both classes at the same time. Still other assignments might be ways students can draw upon knowledge from one course in another, or use work product from one course as raw material for a project in the other.

Reflection Questions

- Which assignment seems the most feasible for your course right now? Why?
- Which assignment seems the most exciting? What would you need to do to prepare yourself to give this assignment? For example, would you need

to sequence the two courses differently? Obtain supplies? Learn about a particular topic? Learn a skill? Get help?

- Which assignments would *not* work for your course? What does that tell you about the values you want to bring to your course? To multidisciplinary projects?

- How was the discussion itself? How did it feel to do this work with your colleague? Regardless of whether you came up with an idea for a multidisciplinary project, why was the discussion still worthwhile?

Variations

If multiple people teach the same course, you can do this protocol as a larger group. Let's say a seventh-grade team has two history teachers and two math teachers. They could simply do this protocol as a group of four, or each history teacher could partner with a different math teacher. The two pairs would use the same assignments and keywords but brainstorm different assignments and then compare notes.

You can also make assignment mashups by yourself. All you need are two assignments, one of your own and one from another course. You won't have the benefit of another person's perspective, and you might come up with assignments that would fit into your colleague's course but not yours—which could leave you feeling frustrated. However, you might come up with a good way to upcycle work product from your colleague's course in yours, or to draw upon knowledge your students bring from other disciplines. If nothing else, this exercise might help you imagine new types of meaningful work your students can do in your course.

Participation Invitation

If you start thinking about interdisciplinary or multidisciplinary curriculum, you might come up with ideas that involve other people's courses and not just your own. But if you simply share your idea, your colleagues might not be as excited about it as you are, because they didn't participate in developing it. They might be supportive, and they might offer suggestions, but that doesn't necessarily mean that they're willing to run with your idea in their classes..

Rather than creating a sales pitch for your colleagues, you can invite them to participate. For this protocol, one person or group (the "presenter") describes an idea to their colleagues (the "listeners"). Then the listeners brainstorm possible ways they could participate. Instead of immediately saying whether they'll participate, the listeners set a date for deciding so that they have time to consider possibilities—just as the presenters had time to formulate their ideas.

In considering ways to participate, the listener uses categories of participation that come from Nina Simon's *The Participatory Museum* (2010): creating, critiquing, collecting, joining, and observing. In explaining these categories, Simon offers the example of participating on YouTube, not just by creating videos but also by leaving comments and ratings, making playlists, subscribing to channels, and sharing links.

Importantly, in Simon's taxonomy, no type of participation is *better* than another. She points out that getting more people to create videos wouldn't make YouTube a better experience for anyone: viewers would have to look through more videos to find what they want, and not everyone has an idea for a video or the skills to make one (Simon, 2010).

We can apply this same reasoning when asking teachers to participate in units that cross disciplines. As with YouTube, asking *more* teachers to create content won't necessarily lead to a *better* learning experience for students; it might just give them more content to wade through. Some teachers might notice how their subject connects but might not be able to think of specific lessons or assignments that would be worth their students' time and lead to meaningful learning. In other words, creating more content—whether for YouTube or a unit—does not necessarily improve anyone's experience and might make their experience worse if it subverts their values.

When you present your idea to your colleagues, offering them different, equally good ways they might participate opens more possibilities for authentic collaboration that can ultimately benefit students. They'll brainstorm ways of participating by answering questions, which appear on the cards in figure 8.7 (p. 179). The cards allow you to shuffle the questions and ask them in any order, so that no form of participation seems more desirable or important than another. To prepare for the protocol, you'll need just one set of cards, cut apart, for the group. You'll also need enough writing supplies so that each group member can take their own notes.

Group Protocol

1. Gather your materials: one set of Participation Question Cards for the group (copied from figure 8.7, p. 179, and cut apart), and writing materials for each person.

CREATING

What lessons or assignments can you imagine creating for your students so they can study this topic as part of your course?

CRITIQUING

How can you imagine giving feedback to students on the work they do in other courses for this unit? How can that feedback reflect your perspective as a teacher of your discipline?

COLLECTING

When do you think about what students will do for this unit in their other courses, what can you imagine collecting? (Words? Images? Ideas? Objects? Something else?) What might you do with that collection?

JOINING

When you think about the work students will do for this unit, which assignments can you imagine doing alongside them? How might your students benefit from seeing you, as a teacher of your discipline, do this work?

OBSERVING

When you imagine the lessons that will be part of this unit in your colleagues' courses, which ones can you imagine observing? How might your observations help your teaching, your colleagues' teaching, or your students' learning?

FIGURE 8.7
Participation Question Cards

2. Shuffle the question cards and place them facedown.
3. The person or group who conceived of an idea for crossing disciplines (the "presenter") describes the work they want to do. Include the values it serves (consulting appendix A on p. 187 if necessary) and how you came up with the idea. You might talk about specific lessons, assignments, field trips, and resources you plan to use. All other group members (the "listeners") silently take notes.
4. The listeners take a few moments to reflect on what they heard. They can ask the presenter any clarifying questions but do not make any statements

of judgment, positive or negative. At this point, the presenter only answers the listeners' questions and makes no suggestions for how the listeners could participate.

5. One listener turns over the top card, and then each listener takes a turn responding to the card's question. If a listener doesn't have an answer to the question, they can pass or say something like "I would need to think more about that." The presenter takes notes on the listeners' responses. When all listeners have answered the first card's question, they turn over the next card and respond to its question while the presenter continues to take notes. This process continues until the listeners have responded to all of the questions in the deck.

6. The presenter takes a few moments to reflect on what they heard.

7. The presenter shares any additional ideas for how the listeners potentially could participate.

8. The entire group sets a time frame during which the listeners will decide whether and how they want to participate in the unit. The time frame should provide enough time for the listeners to make a decision comfortably but not so much time that the presenter won't be able to proceed and plan.

Reflection Questions

- If you were a presenter, how did it feel to share your ideas? To answer questions? To hold back comments while the listeners shared their ideas? If any of this was hard, why was it still worthwhile?

- If you were a listener, how did it feel to hear your colleague's ideas? To ask questions about it? To share your own ideas? If any of this was hard, why was it still worthwhile?

- How did it feel to wait to make a decision rather than making a decision right away? Why is waiting worthwhile?

- What did you appreciate about each colleague you had this conversation with?

- How do you feel about yourself as a result of having this conversation?

Variation

Using question cards might seem a little silly, but the cards have two important purposes. First, because you can shuffle them and ask the questions in any order, you aren't leading with or building up to any particular form of participation. Instead, all forms have equal weight. Second, seeing the questions one at a time means that you can give each one your full attention and take your time to think of an answer, instead of mentally skipping ahead to an easier or more exciting question. All of that said, if you use this protocol with just two people—one presenter and one listener—the cards might seem a little awkward. In that case, you can just use the questions in figure 8.7 (p. 179) without turning them into cards, and the listener can answer the questions in any order.

ONWARD

In this chapter, we saw ways you can create connections between disciplines. Although inquiries, projects, and even individual learning tasks become more complex as you involve more people and perspectives, that burden is shared, and if nothing else, building something meaningful together strengthens relationships. Those relationships can sustain and empower you as you strive to teach more meaningful units, whether collaboratively or on your own.

Conclusion

The Teacher You Want to Be

This book has a grammatically incorrect title. *Teach Meaningful?* The author taught English for many years. If one of her students had written *teach meaningful*, she would have commented, *Teach meaningful WHAT?* Yes, in all caps. Then she probably would've planned a lesson on how adjectives always modify nouns.

But as someone who is constantly learning about curriculum design and values work, the author intentionally left this book's title as an incomplete thought. That's because what constitutes *meaningful* teaching is always changing.

For one thing, a new unit will create unexpected challenges. Due to the complex interdependent relationships within a system (such as a school), a small change to one part (a unit) will have ripple effects. Students who learn in math to analyze the distribution of fresh produce in the Bronx might wonder in history class about the distribution of resources in Mesopotamia. Students who do service learning by writing Spanish-language pamphlets about preparing for emergencies might need to say things such as "You should buy enough water to last for three days," and now they need lessons on the subjunctive. Any change will have unintended consequences, and your values can help you decide how to respond.

Another reason you'll never finish working on your units is that you'll do an incomplete job aligning them to your values. A unit of study is always a compromise between multiple values within the confines of time. Some math teachers say they value giving real-life problems but that they also value teaching skills for mastery, and they don't have time to do both as well as they'd like. Art teachers who value teaching a process might wonder if their students create enough products or feel that the products aren't of high enough quality. You might be unhappy with the way you prioritize your values one year and take corrective action the next year.

Even if you anticipate every outcome and find the perfect balance between your values, the work of designing values-congruent curriculum still won't be done. Your students always will be different, asking new questions and throwing you new challenges. Your colleagues will share ideas that push and inspire you. Articles and workshops will bump up against the ways you teach or give you new insights you want to act on. Even events in your personal life, movies you watch, stories you hear, things you notice on walks and in conversations—they'll all come back to haunt your perfectly aligned units.

The world you teach about is also changing. Curriculum design consultant Heidi Hayes Jacobs (2010) borrows the term *upgrading* from the information technology field to describe how teachers make learning more relevant for our times by replacing dated assignments (such as oral reports) with more contemporary ones (such as TED talks), embedding media and cultural literacy skills, and rethinking content in light of our rapidly changing world. Every day, scientists make discoveries, history unfolds, and artists produce new work. The world's knowledge base and problems are growing exponentially. How can your units remain the same?

Education professor James McKernan (2008) imagines "a curriculum conceived not as a final and prescriptive solution, but as a set of hypotheses" (p. 115), and that the people best positioned to test these hypotheses aren't outside researchers but teachers. *You* have the professional judgment to interrogate the curriculum, and *you* have the expertise to change it. You can study how well your curriculum works—the extent to which its results match your shifting values. Keep asking questions about your own practice, collecting and analyzing your own data, and using that data to make decisions. The exercises and protocols in this book can become routine practices you use to continually reassess and reimagine your curriculum.

Another way you can continuously rethink your teaching in terms of your values is to identify supportive colleagues who reflect back your excitement when you talk through a new unit, push back when you make self-limiting statements, provoke you with their insights, and help you hold yourself accountable to your goals. You might leave these conversations surprised by your own successes, impressed by your colleagues' insights into your work, and ready to revise your units. It can be an immensely powerful experience to have colleagues see your work and recognize the things you value in it.

Finally, you can maintain the energy it takes to keep working on your curriculum by seeking professional development that matches your values as a teacher. If you see a professional learning opportunity—a book, lecture, workshop, or conference, or something within your school such as a peer observation group or a lunch-and-learn discussion—it's less important that the topic matches your curriculum than that the underlying values match your own. As long as you go into the experience with openness and curiosity, a connection to your curriculum will present itself eventually, and sometimes immediately.

Back in the '80s, in a commercial for milk, a girl complained about her appearance to her increasingly older self in the mirror. The older girl encouraged her younger self by showing her how beautiful and confident she eventually would become (with a little help from milk, of course). If you can get past this commercial's problematic message that girls can only be happy if they're pretty, you might like the idea of envisioning the person you'll become and imagining the encouraging words that person might say to you in moments when you're struggling.

When you imagine the teacher you want to be, what does that person do? What does their classroom look like? What are the students doing? If this teacher could speak to you, what kind words would they offer when you struggle? What would they say to remind you of what really matters?

Let's end there, not with the author's words of encouragement, but with your own.

Appendix A

Examples of Values

Below is a list of qualities some people find important to bring to their actions. Which ones do you think are important to bring to your teaching? Your relationships with students and colleagues? Which ones do you think are important for your students to bring to their learning, work, and interactions in your classroom?

Accountability	Determination	Innovation	Presence
Accuracy	Directness	Integrity	Productivity
Activity	Easiness	Intelligence	Prudence
Agility	Efficiency	Involvement	Reliability
Appreciation	Effort	Joy	Resilience
Approachability	Empathy	Judgment	Resourcefulness
Authenticity	Enthusiasm	Justice	Respect
Autonomy	Excellence	Kindness	Responsibility
Awareness	Expertise	Knowledge	Responsiveness
Boldness	Faith	Loyalty	Restraint
Clarity	Flexibility	Mastery	Self-awareness
Closeness	Freedom	Modesty	Simplicity
Collaboration	Generosity	Openness	Sincerity
Commitment	Gratitude	Optimism	Stability
Compassion	Helpfulness	Orderliness	Sustainability
Connection	Honesty	Organization	Tact
Cooperation	Hope	Patience	Thoroughness
Courage	Humor	Peace	Trustworthiness
Creativity	Imagination	Persistence	Variety
Curiosity	Inclusivity	Perspective	Versatility
Dedication	Independence	Playfulness	Warmth
Deference	Individuality	Practicality	Wisdom

Appendix B

Types of Meaningful Work

The chart that follows classifies real-world work products in two ways. First, it distinguishes between *things*, which exist in space; and *events*, which exist in time. Next, it distinguishes between *approximated* and *simulated* work. When creating approximated work products, students authentically make something that exists in the real world but are not ready or required to meet professional standards. For example, students putting on a play to dramatize the cell cycle probably wouldn't need to consider set and lighting design—because the play itself is not so much the point as the learning students would derive from creating it. They're *approximating* a play.

Students writing poems for a high-school English class might more closely approximate published poetry, and some students might write poems of publishable quality. But the teacher might specify certain conditions that don't exist in the real world (such as that students have to use iambic pentameter) and remove other conditions that do (such as that students do *not* have to write poems that do something original with language, because the learning goal isn't so much inventiveness as fluency). In cases such as these, students are coming as close as they can to real-world work while also fulfilling certain learning objectives.

Simulations intentionally include an element of roleplay or a suspension of disbelief. When students write poems for an English class, they really are writing poems, but if they put a book character on trial, they're pretending. In

	Things		Events	
Approximated	Animation	Map	Art exhibition	Poster presentation
	Blog	Model	Awareness campaign	Protest
	Board game	Newsletter	Banquet	Recitation
	Bot	Painting	Concert/recital	Reenactment
	Budget	Personal essay	Experiment	Song
	Chart	Petition	Game	Spoken word
	Collage	Photo essay	Guided tour	Talk
	Comic	Picture book	How-to demonstration	
	Diagram	Poem	Interactive timeline	
	Documentary	Review (of an event, book, product, etc.)	Interview	
	Field journal	Script	Lesson	
	Graph	Toy	Play	
	Letter to a decision-maker	Website		
Simulated	Advertisement	Op-ed	Awards ceremony	Restorative justice circle
	Article	Photo album/stream	Board meeting	Sales pitch
	Blueprint	Proposal (as for goods or services)	Campaign speech	Talk show
	Brochure	Resumé	Convention	Trial/hearing
	Business plan	Social media profile	Crime scene	
	Catalog	Soundtrack	Eulogy (for a person or idea)	
	Diary	Travel log	Focus group	
	Fashion design		Job interview	
	Letter to a literary or historical figure		Museum	
	Menu		Panel discussion	
	Newspaper		Podcast	

FIGURE B1
Types of Meaningful Work
Adapted from Porosoff & Weinstein, 2020.

simulations, students create a temporary world where they are not themselves and can use the knowledge and skills they learned in school in ways they wouldn't otherwise have access to. As attorneys putting a book character on trial, students can practice gathering textual evidence, making a claim, listening, and thinking critically in ways that simultaneously invoke the real world and their imaginations, and that feel at once serious and playful.

Works Cited

Bennett, R., & Oliver, J. (2019). *Acceptance and commitment therapy: 100 key points and techniques.* New York: Routledge.

Berger, R. (2013). Deeper learning: Highlighting student work. *Edutopia.* Retrieved August 3, 2019, from https://www.edutopia.org/blog/deeper-learning-student -work-ron-berger

Bishop, R. S. (1990). Mirrors, windows, and sliding glass doors. *Perspectives: Choosing and Using Books for the Classroom, 6(3).*

Blackledge, J. T. (2015). *Cognitive defusion in practice: A clinician's guide to assessing, observing, and supporting change in your client.* Oakland, CA: New Harbinger.

Brophy, J., & Alleman, J. (1991). A caveat: Curriculum integration isn't always a good idea. *Educational Leadership, 42(2),* 66.

Bryan, J. (2012). *From the dress-up corner to the senior prom: Navigating gender and sexuality diversity in preK–12 schools.* Lanham, MD: Rowman & Littlefield Education.

Bryson, B. (2004). *A short history of nearly everything.* New York, NY: Broadway Books.

Cisneros, S. (1991). *The house on Mango Street.* New York, NY: Vintage.

Dahl, J., Lundgren, T., Plumb, J., & Stewart, I. (2009). *The art and science of valuing in psychotherapy: Helping clients discover, explore, and commit to valued action using acceptance and commitment therapy.* Oakland, CA: New Harbinger.

Daniels, H. (1994). *Literature circles: Voice and choice in the student-centered classroom.* Portsmouth, NH: Stenhouse.

Erickson, H. L. (1998). *Concept-based curriculum and instruction: Teaching beyond the facts.* Thousand Oaks, CA: Corwin.

Fluckiger, J. (2010). Single point rubric: A tool for responsible student self-assessment. *Delta Kappa Gamma Bulletin, 76*(4), 18.

Fogarty, R. (1991). *How to integrate the curricula.* Palatine, IL: Skylight.

Geist, E. (2010). The anti-anxiety curriculum: Combating math anxiety in the classroom. *Journal of Instructional Psychology, 37*(1).

Gilbert, P. (2010). *The compassionate mind: A new approach to life's challenges.* Oakland, CA: New Harbinger.

Gober, R. (1989). Untitled [Installation found in Art Institute Chicago, Chicago, IL]. Retrieved June 6, 2019, from https://www.artic.edu/artists/55184/robert-gober

Graham, P. (2009, July). Maker's Schedule, Manager's Schedule. Retrieved August 14, 2019, from http://www.paulgraham.com/makersschedule.html

Graham, S., & Perin, D. (2007). A meta-analysis of writing instruction for adolescent students. *Journal of Educational Psychology, 99*(3), 445–476.

Guskey, T. R. (2015). *On your mark: Challenging the conventions of grading and reporting.* Bloomington, IN: Solution Tree.

Hansberry, L. (1994). *A raisin in the sun.* New York, NY: Vintage. (Original work published 1959)

Harris, R. (2009). *ACT made simple: An easy-to-read primer on acceptance and commitment therapy.* Oakland, CA: New Harbinger.

Hayes, S. C. (Ed.). (1989). *Rule-governed behavior: Cognition, contingencies, and instructional control.* New York, NY: Plenum Press.

Hayes, S. C., Strosahl, K. D., & Wilson, K. G. (2012). *Acceptance and commitment therapy: The process and practice of mindful change.* New York, NY: Guilford.

House, S., & Vaswani, N. (2012). *Same sun here.* Somerville, MA: Candlewick Press.

Jacobs, H. H. (2010). *Curriculum 21: Essential education for a changing world.* Alexandria, VA: ASCD.

Karpicke, J. D., & Blunt, J. R. (2011). Retrieval practice produces more learning than elaborative studying with concept mapping. *Science, 331* (6018), 772–775.

Krathwohl, D. R. (2002). A revision of Bloom's taxonomy: An overview. *Theory into Practice, 41*(4), 212–218.

Kaufman, M. (2014). *The Laramie project.* New York, NY: Vintage.

Lyon, G. E. (1999). Where I'm from. In *Where I'm from: Where poems come from* (p. 3). Spring, TX: Absey.

Martinez, S. L., & Stager, G. (2013). *Invent to learn: Making, tinkering, and engineering in the classroom.* Torrance, CA: Constructing Modern Knowledge.

Maslow, A. H. (1943). A theory of human motivation. *Psychological Review, 50*(4), 370.

McDonough, W., & Braungart, M. (2002). *Cradle to cradle: Remaking the way we make things.* New York, NY: North Point.

McDonough, W., & Braungart, M. (2013). *The upcycle: Beyond sustainability—designing for abundance.* New York, NY: North Point.

McKernan, J. (2008). *Curriculum and imagination: Process theory, pedagogy and action research.* London: Routledge.

McTighe, J., & Wiggins, G. (2013). *Essential questions: Opening doors to student understanding.* Alexandria, VA: ASCD.

Meadows, D. H. (2008). *Thinking in systems: A primer.* White River Junction, VT: Chelsea Green.

Moncton, K. (2009). Curriculum: Visual & cultural backgrounds through the art of Robert Grober. *Teachers for Social Justice.* Retrieved June 6, 2019, from http://www.teachersforjustice.org/2009/09/curriculum-visual-cultural-backgrounds.html

Muir, J. (2004). *My first summer in the Sierra.* Mineola, NY: Dover. (Original work published 1911)

National Governors Association Center for Best Practices and Council of Chief State School Officers (2012). Frequently asked questions. *Common Core state standards initiative.* Retrieved March 23, 2018, from http://www.corestandards .org/resources/frequently-asked-questions

Nelson, M. (2001). *Carver: A life in poems.* Honesdale, PA: Front Street.

Newell, W. H. (2013). The state of the field: Interdisciplinary theory. *Issues in Interdisciplinary Studies, 31*, 22–43.

Newell, W. H., & Green, W. J. (1982). Defining and teaching interdisciplinary studies. *Improving College and University Teaching, 30*(1), 23–30.

Nitko, A. J., & Brookhart, S. M. (2007). *Educational assessment of students* (5th ed.). Upper Saddle River, NJ: Pearson Prentice Hall.

NYU Music Experience Design Lab (2017). Groove Pizza (Version 2.0) [Mobile application software]. Retrieved September 29, 2019, from https://apps.musedlab .org/groovepizza/

Okorafor, N. (2017). *Akata witch*. New York, NY: Penguin.

Page, K., & Dornenburg, A. (2008). *The flavor bible: The essential guide to culinary creativity, based on the wisdom of America's most imaginative chefs*. Boston, MA: Little, Brown.

Paschen, E., & Raccah, D. (2010). *Poetry speaks who I am*. Naperville, IL: Jabberwocky.

Pink, D. H. (2006). *A whole new mind: Why right-brainers will rule the future*. New York, NY: Riverhead.

Poe, E. A. (2008). Annabel Lee. In *The complete poetry of Edgar Allan Poe* (pp. 116–117). New York, NY: Penguin. (Original work published 1849)

Porosoff, L., & Weinstein, J. (2020). *Two-for-one teaching: Connecting instruction to student values*. Bloomington, IN: Solution Tree.

Powell, K. (2019). *Boredom busters: Transform worksheets, lectures, and grading into engaging, meaningful learning experiences*. Dave Burgess Consulting.

Ruhlman, M. (2009). *Ratio: The simple codes behind the craft of everyday cooking*. New York, NY: Simon & Schuster.

Satrapi, M. (2003). *Persepolis*. New York, NY: Pantheon.

Schiro, M. (2013). Introduction to the curriculum ideologies. In *Curriculum theory: Conflicting visions and enduring concerns* (pp. 1–14). Thousand Oaks, CA: Sage.

Siedentop, D. L., Hastie, P., & Van der Mars, H. (2004). *Complete guide to sport education*. Champaign, IL: Human Kinetics.

Simon, N. (2010). *The participatory museum*. Santa Cruz, CA: Museum 2.0.

Skloot, R. (2017). *The immortal life of Henrietta Lacks.* New York, NY: Broadway Books.

Sleeter, C. E. (2005). *Un-standardizing curriculum: Multicultural teaching in the standards-based classroom.* New York, NY: Teachers College Press.

Steinbeck, J. (1993). *Of mice and men.* New York, NY: Penguin. (Original work published 1937)

Stewart, I., Barnes-Holmes, D., Hayes, S. C., & Lipkens, R. (2001). Relations among relations: Analogies, metaphors, and stories. In S. C. Hayes, D. Barnes-Holmes, & B. Roche (Eds.). *Relational frame theory: A post-Skinnerian account of human language and cognition* (pp. 73–86). New York, NY: Kluwer Academic/Plenum.

Style, E. (1988). Curriculum as window and mirror. *Listening for All Voices: Gender Balancing the School Curriculum,* 6–12.

Sweeney, L. B. (2001) *When a butterfly sneezes: A guide for helping kids explore interconnections in our world through favorite stories.* Waltham, MA: Pegasus Communications.

Tieben, R., Sturm, J., Bekker, T., & Schouten, B. (2014). Playful persuasion: Designing for ambient playful interactions in public spaces. *Journal of Ambient Intelligence and Smart Environments, 6*(4), 341–357.

Tirch, D., Silberstein, L. R., & Kolts, R. L. (2015). *Buddhist psychology and cognitive-behavioral therapy: A clinician's guide.* New York, NY: Guilford.

Tokuhama-Espinosa, T. (2011). *Mind, brain, and education science: A comprehensive guide to the new brain-based teaching.* New York, NY: W. W. Norton.

Turner, E. E., & Font Strawhun, B. T. (2007). Posing problems that matter: Investigating school overcrowding. *Teaching Children Mathematics, 13*(9), 457–463.

University of Chicago School Mathematics Project. (2007). *Everyday mathematics grade 2: Teacher's lesson guide* (3rd ed., Vol. 1, *Everyday mathematics*). Chicago, IL: McGraw-Hill.

Villatte, M., Villatte, J. L., & Hayes, S. C. (2016). *Mastering the clinical conversation: Language as intervention.* New York, NY: Guilford.

Wiggins, G. P., & McTighe, J. (2005). *Understanding by design* (2nd ed.). Alexandria, VA: ASCD.

Wiggins, G. P., & McTighe, J. (2007). *Schooling by design: Mission, action, and achievement*. Alexandria, VA: ASCD.

Willis, J. (2011). A neurologist makes the case for the video game model as a learning tool. *Edutopia*. Retrieved August 7, 2019, from http://www.edutopia .org/blog/video-games-learning-student-engagement-judy-willis

Wilson, K. G., & DuFrene, T. (2009). *Mindfulness for two: An acceptance and commitment therapy approach to mindfulness in psychotherapy*. Oakland, CA: New Harbinger.

Wilson, K. G., & Murell, A. R. (2004). Values work in acceptance and commitment therapy: Setting a course for behavioral treatment. In S. C. Hayes, V. M. Follette, & M. M. Linehan (Eds.), *Mindfulness and acceptance: Expanding the cognitive-behavioral tradition* (pp. 120–151). New York, NY: Guilford.

Wilson, M. (2006). *Rethinking rubrics in writing assessment*. Portsmouth, NH: Heinemann.

Yadavaia, J. E., & Hayes, S. C. (2009). Values in acceptance and commitment therapy: A comparison with four other approaches. *Hellenic Journal of Psychology, 6*, 244–272.

Yezierska, A., & Kessler-Harris, A. (2003). *Bread givers: A Novel*. New York, NY: Persea. (Original work published 1923)

About the Author

Lauren Porosoff has been an educator since 2000, and she writes and presents about how to design curriculum and professional development that empowers students and teachers. Informed by research and practices from contextual behavioral science, Lauren has developed novel approaches to making schoolwork meaningful. She and her husband, Jonathan Weinstein, coauthored *EMPOWER Your Students: Tools to Inspire a Meaningful School Experience* (2018) and *Two-for-One Teaching: Connecting Instruction to Student Values* (2020). Lauren also has written articles for *AMLE Magazine*, *Independent School*, *Phi Delta Kappan*, the PBS NewsHour blog, *Rethinking Schools*, and *Teaching Tolerance* about how students and teachers can clarify and commit to their values at school. To learn more about Lauren's work, visit her EMPOWER Forwards website (empowerforwards.com) and follow her on Twitter at @LaurenPorosoff.

Made in the USA
Middletown, DE
26 October 2021